T0063850

THE SOCIAL SURVIVAL GUIDE FOR TEENS ON THE AUTISM SPECTRUM

THE
SOCIAL SURVIVAL
GUIDE FOR TEENS
ON THE AUTISM SPECTRUM

How to Make Friends
and Navigate Your Emotions

Lindsey Sterling, PhD

**ROCKRIDGE
PRESS**

Copyright © 2020 by Rockridge Press, Emeryville, California

No part of this publication may be reproduced, stored in a retrieval system, or transmitted in any form or by any means, electronic, mechanical, photocopying, recording, scanning, or other-wise, except as permitted under Sections 107 or 108 of the 1976 United States Copyright Act, without the prior written permission of the Publisher. Requests to the Publisher for permission should be addressed to the Permissions Department, Rockridge Press, 6005 Shellmound Street, Suite 175, Emeryville, CA 94608.

Limit of Liability/Disclaimer of Warranty: The Publisher and the author make no representa-tions or warranties with respect to the accuracy or completeness of the contents of this work and specifically disclaim all warranties, including without limitation warranties of fitness for a particular purpose. No warranty may be created or extended by sales or promotional materials. The advice and strategies contained herein may not be suitable for every situation. This work is sold with the understanding that the Publisher is not engaged in rendering medical, legal, or other professional advice or services. If professional assistance is required, the services of a competent professional person should be sought. Neither the Publisher nor the author shall be liable for damages arising herefrom. The fact that an individual, organization, or website is referred to in this work as a citation and/or potential source of further information does not mean that the author or the Publisher endorses the information the individual, organization, or website may provide or recommendations they/it may make. Further, readers should be aware that websites listed in this work may have changed or disappeared between when this work was written and when it is read.

For general information on our other products and services or to obtain technical support, please contact our Customer Care Department within the United States at (866) 744-2665, or outside the United States at (510) 253-0500.

Rockridge Press publishes its books in a variety of electronic and print formats. Some content that appears in print may not be available in electronic books, and vice versa.

TRADEMARKS: Rockridge Press and the Rockridge Press logo are trademarks or registered trademarks of Callisto Media Inc. and/or its affiliates, in the United States and other countries, and may not be used without written permission. All other trademarks are the property of their respective owners. Rockridge Press is not associated with any product or vendor mentioned in this book.

Interior and Cover Designer: Michael Cook
Art Producer: Hannah Dickerson
Editor: Annie Choi
Production Editor: Matt Burnett

All illustrations and photography used under license from Shutterstock.com and iStock.com

ISBN: Print 978-1-64739-010-5 | eBook 978-1-64739-011-2
R0

Dedicated to my boys, Jackson and Levi,
who wanted to see Mommy's book.
I hope I made you proud.

CONTENTS

INTRODUCTION

If you have a tough time navigating social situations, you are not alone. Social interactions can be downright tricky and uncomfortable. If you are on the autism spectrum or if you have learning or thinking differences, social situations can be even more difficult to navigate.

This book is designed to guide you through these situations. The purpose of this book is to give you the skills you need to handle different social situations *if* and *when* you want to. If your goal is to make new friends or strengthen existing friendships, this book can help you feel more comfortable working toward those goals.

About This Book

This book is based on more than 20 years of my research and experience working with people on the autism spectrum, including 10 years as a licensed clinical psychologist. In my private practice in Southern California, I have the privilege of working with autistic children, teens, and adults and their families on a daily basis. I continue to learn new things from them every day. They have been my continual teachers in understanding autism spectrum disorder (ASD) and have given me the insight needed to write this book.

This book is divided into three parts:

Part 1: Getting Started reviews basic communication tips and explores how thoughts and feelings work, so you can understand your own mental and emotional responses better.

Part 2: Taking Care of Yourself covers how to manage your own emotions so you can feel more comfortable when connecting with others.

Part 3: Social Survival Guide shows you how to interact with others in common social scenarios.

This book will give you strategies to help manage anxiety and other emotions that can interfere with your social experiences. Becoming familiar with these strategies will help you feel more confident in social situations and build healthy friendships. While the book is meant to be read from start to finish, feel free to flip to the sections most relevant to you!

The Book's Approach

Most of the strategies in this book have been shown to be helpful for autistic people in my clinical practice and in studies by other researchers. That means that real people have tried them in real-world situations, and they've worked. Many of the strategies described in part 2 were influenced by the work of Dr. Jeffrey Wood, whose research focuses on the use of cognitive behavioral therapy (CBT) to target symptoms of anxiety in autistic youth. Dr. Elizabeth Laugeson's Program for Education and Enrichment of Relational Skills (PEERS) has also influenced my clinical practice and some of the tips provided in this book.

How to Use This Book

This purpose of this book is not to label you as a person with social challenges, to determine whether you are autistic, or to identify where you fall on the spectrum. Instead, this book is meant to walk you through social interactions in a fun, supportive way.

Each chapter includes Check-In questions that introduce the topics you'll explore. They are optional, but I recommend spending 5 to 10 minutes thinking about them or discussing with a trusted adult in order to get the most out of each chapter. Use the Exercises and step-by-step guides to practice for different social scenarios. Use the Reflection Questions to start thinking about how to apply your new skills to real-life scenarios.

While some of the strategies may work for teens with challenges like social anxiety, the difficulties you face as an autistic teen may be unique, due to complications with interpreting subtle social cues like reading facial expression or tone of voice. You may also be carrying with you a history of repeated negative social interactions that has impacted how you view and approach new experiences. Although the book is written with older kids and teens in mind, most of the ideas can also apply to young adults.

Note that this book uses identity-first language ("autistic teen") rather than person-first language ("teen with autism") to refer to people on the autism spectrum. This is to reflect the book's empowering and holistic approach, not to dictate what term you should be using.

There is no one right way to approach ASD because no two autistic people are the same. Each person has a unique personality, with strengths and challenges of their own. The skills outlined in this book will apply to many people on the autism spectrum, but you can pick and choose what works best for you.

Let's get started!

PART ONE

GETTING STARTED

Good communication skills make it easier to connect with others and build friendships. Part 1 will help you navigate the basics of communication. We'll explore the benefits of friendships and how to identify potential friends. You'll review verbal and nonverbal communication and get tips for understanding subtler messages like sarcasm. You'll explore how your emotions affect communication so that you can better interpret the messages other people might be sending and feel more comfortable expressing yourself.

CHAPTER ONE

WHAT ARE FRIENDS FOR, ANYWAY?

We all have different reasons for socializing. How much time we like to be around others differs from person to person, too. Some of us recharge in a group, and some of us need more alone time. But we all want to feel like we have the skills to interact with others and make friends if and when we want to. In this chapter, you'll explore how to identify potential friends and determine what kind of community you want to build for yourself.

Before you dive in, ask yourself:
- What qualities do you want in a friend?
- How can you tell if someone is your friend?
- What's a potential benefit of forming a close friendship?

Why Friends Matter

So many events in life, like family get-togethers, going to the movies, or working on a group project, involve some sort of social interaction. Some sports, board games, and video games require more than one person to play. Sometimes you need someone to confide in when something stressful happens. Other times, you just want to share your happiness with others. Friendship allows us to share experiences *with* someone else.

Having a friend can make stressful experiences easier to navigate. Friendships have been proven to be good for our physical and mental health. They help reduce stress and anxiety and even reduce risk for things like depression down the road.

A good friend can provide support and make us feel like we belong to a bigger community, whether at school, on a team, or at work. Having a friend can even make it easier to make new friends. Isn't it easier to approach a group when you are with a friend rather than on your own?

Finding Your People

There are no rules that say how many friends you should have or how social you should be. You might feel satisfied with one close friend, and someone else might feel comfortable having four or five. This is something you define for yourself as you learn over time what makes you feel fulfilled.

Although you might be drawn to a person who seems popular, consider what qualities you actually want in a potential friend.

After all, just because someone might be a great friend to other people doesn't mean they will be the best fit for you.

What Makes a Friend?

A friend usually shares some common interests or activities with you. But when you don't have obvious things in common with someone, you might still want to be friends because of that person's positive qualities. A person who is loyal, nonjudgmental, kind, trustworthy, and honest will probably be a good choice. For example, someone who shows concern for others, stands up for others when they need help, and doesn't lie might make a good friend.

A potential friend should show interest in wanting to be your friend, too. For example, if the interest is reciprocal, you take turns starting conversations and making plans to hang out. You return each other's texts or calls. If a friendship is not reciprocal, one person might view the friendship differently or not contribute as much to the relationship.

Friends help us feel connected and less alone. They remind us that we are surrounded by others who share similar goals or interests, which boosts positive emotions. In a healthy friendship, you should feel good and appreciated!

When we follow someone on social media, we get a front-row view into their personal lives, but we can also feel a false sense of familiarity. For example, we get to see their family or daily activities, even though we barely talk to them in person. On social media, we also pick and choose what to post, which doesn't reflect what life is really like.

It's important to distinguish following someone from a true friendship, which is reciprocal and based on common interests. Most importantly, friendships tend to develop from face-to-face conversation and activities shared in real life, not just virtually. A friend knows your in-person persona as well as your online persona, and accepts and supports you both in person and online. We generally place greater value on real-life friendships and form a deeper connection with our friends than with our followers.

If someone follows you on social media, make sure you know who they are before you let them see your profile. Ask yourself: "Have I met this person before? Do we have friends in common?" When you allow them to follow you, remember that this person now has access to your comments, pictures, and online persona.

Who Isn't a Friend?

As you consider what characteristics to look for in a friend, it's also important to know what traits and behaviors you *don't* want in a friend. Pay attention to how you feel when you are with the other person. Does your mood improve as a result of being with the person, or do you feel worse? Trust your feelings.

In addition to paying attention to your gut feelings about a person, watch the things they say or do. Be wary of someone who seems to take advantage of you. For example, think twice about people who only call or text you when they need something, put you down in front of others, or violate your trust in some way. If you have confided something personal to your friend and they reveal it to someone else, they have violated your trust.

Also think carefully about people who dominate conversations or are overly competitive. When someone asks you what grade you got on a test or how many friends you have on social media, for example, they may be comparing themselves and trying to compete with you rather than being happy for you.

We also have to be careful about trusting a friend *too* much. Unfortunately, some friends can become envious of our achievements, put us down in front of others, or betray us in some other way. We all make mistakes, but if you see that this is a pattern in one of your friends, you should consider whether you want to keep hanging out with them.

What to Expect from Friends

Friends can play a variety of roles in our lives. How do we know which friend to text when we are feeling down? Whom do we call when we want to share something funny that just happened? And how do we know how often to reach out to any one of our friends?

In friendships, we have to be realistic about what we can expect from any one person. For example, your closest friend may have *other* close friends and may not be available to you all the time, and that's okay. When it comes to dating, the roles can seem clearer because typically *one* primary person fulfills the role of boyfriend or girlfriend.

Here are some different roles friends can play in our lives:

- Best friend or confidant
- Hobby companion
- Support system
- Study or running partner
- Lunch or snack buddy
- Video game partner
- Teammate

It's okay for friends to play different roles and to be different from us. It's probably more interesting that way! If we put too much pressure on one person to fulfill every role, we may be let down.

Friends Make Mistakes, Too

Sometimes even your best friends can let you down by saying something mean or leaving you out, making you feel sad or disappointed. Even when friends let you down, you might want to give them the benefit of the doubt initially. This means that you assume they have good intentions even when you're not sure.

When you give people the benefit of the doubt, you can help clear up misunderstandings. For example, ask for clarification if you're not sure why your friend said something to you. This gives them a chance to share their perspective. You might learn that there was a good reason for what your friend did.

You can also share how their actions made you feel. In chapter 2, you'll learn how to do this in more detail. If they're a good friend, they will try to understand where you're coming from. Just because your friend made a mistake, that does not automatically make them a bad person, unless they continue to be hurtful.

▶ REFLECTION QUESTIONS

- What makes you want to connect with others socially?
- Have the qualities you want in a friend changed at all after reading this chapter?

CHAPTER TWO

COMMUNICATION BASICS

We communicate not just to share information but also to have fun and connect with other people. Communication lets us create and maintain friendships. But sometimes it can feel like a lot of work to figure out what someone *means* when they say something, or if someone is being serious or sarcastic. People also have different communication styles, which can make things more confusing. The good news is that there are strategies you can use to break down these cues! In this chapter, you'll review the basics of verbal and nonverbal communication, and get tips for making sense of some of the less obvious ways people communicate.

Do you relate to these statements?

- I have a good vocabulary and understand the words people use, but I don't always get what they really mean.
- I have a hard time expressing myself in ways others understand.
- I often feel that people misinterpret what I mean.

What Is Communication?

Communication is the transfer of information from one person to another. We share information verbally, nonverbally, in writing, and even visually. You might feel more comfortable with one type of communication than another. For example, Dr. Temple Grandin, a professor of animal science and an autism spokesperson, is famous for "thinking in pictures" rather than in words.

We also communicate electronically via text and email. Many people prefer online communication because they can respond in their own time and on their terms, without the pressure of being put on the spot during a conversation. But online communication doesn't show cues about a person's tone or underlying meaning—even with the best emojis!

Nonverbal Communication

Nonverbal communication can include facial expressions, gaze, gestures, body posture, personal space, tone of voice, inflection, volume, and touch. It provides important information about a person's feelings, which we might miss if we pay attention to their words only.

For example, imagine you run into a classmate after math class, and he says, "I did awesome on that test." Based on his words alone, you might assume that he actually aced the test. But when we consider the nonverbal cues he gave while making the statement, we might get a different picture. For example, if he rolls his eyes, shakes his head, and uses a tone of voice that shows disappointment, he may actually be making a sarcastic statement that shows a lack of confidence.

In fact, most of the messages we receive from others don't come from what they say, but rather from *how* they say it. This means that we need to pay careful attention to nonverbal signs to really understand what others mean.

Eye Contact

Meeting someone's gaze with your own shows a person that you are interested and paying attention. We often make more eye contact when we are listening than when we are talking, but how much time we actually look at someone's eyes during conversation varies from person to person. When making eye contact, it's okay to take breaks. In fact, if you stare at someone intently for more than a few seconds at a time, it can feel too intense for the other person.

Some people struggle with looking at someone directly in the eyes when interacting because it can be overstimulating and anxiety-provoking. If making eye contact feels too uncomfortable for you, check in with your eyes by looking briefly at someone and then away while they are speaking. For example, you could try to make eye contact after every three or four sentences that the other person says. Doing so shows that you are interested and paying attention, even if your gaze is not on the speaker the entire time.

You can also try looking *near* the eyes of the other person, like the forehead area between the eyes, or even at the mouth. Avoid looking at other body parts, especially below the neck, since this might make others feel uncomfortable. Once you get to know a person better, you can share that eye contact is uncomfortable for you, so your friend doesn't misinterpret your avoidance as disinterest.

What do you think each person is trying to communicate?

Answer Key: 1. Bored; 2. Annoyed; 3. Amused; 4. Interested; 5. Friendly

BODY POSTURE	WHAT IT USUALLY MEANS
	Open body language shows that the other person wants to interact.
	Closed body language could mean that the person is feeling defensive, bored, anxious, angry, or unsure of themselves.
	Facing the person and leaning forward shows that you are interested and eager to listen and keep interacting.

It's important to notice another person's eye contact, too. If the other person consistently looks around the room, at their watch, or even at their phone, they may not be interested in continuing the conversation. This is a good time to pause to give them an opportunity to say something or end the conversation.

Facial Expressions

Facial expressions can reveal underlying feelings without any words. Expressions can be subtle and intricate, involving many different facial muscles. Human brains have evolved to quickly recognize faces and facial expressions, and respond to these signals in social situations.

If you have a hard time reading facial expressions, knowing how to respond in the moment can be difficult. Some facial expressions are fleeting, making them challenging to spot and even harder to interpret, especially if eye contact feels like a struggle. If you're confused about someone's facial expressions or if you feel misunderstood, ask for clarification, and provide it for someone else if asked.

Body Language

Posture, or the way a person holds their body, sends information about their feelings or mood. It also sends messages about how open or receptive they are during a social interaction. If they turn their body and face toward someone while that person is speaking, it shows that they are interested and open to listening. If they cross their arms and turn their body away from someone, it suggests that they could be uncomfortable, disinterested, or defensive.

When interacting with someone, you can **mirror** their body language using a similar posture to show the other person you are listening. Mirroring helps build connection with the person you're talking to. For example, if you are sitting across from another person and they are leaning forward and resting their face in their hand while listening, this shows interest. You might also lean forward and model this body language to show that you are interested and engaged in the conversation, too. Note that mirroring someone's body language doesn't mean copying their every move.

Hand Gestures

We use hand gestures while speaking to add emphasis or meaning to the words we are using. An **emphatic gesture** stresses a certain word, idea, or feeling. Someone making an important point might move their hands and arms vigorously as they speak. A **descriptive gesture** gives others a visual of the message being conveyed. For example, if you're telling a friend to meet you under the big arch at the entrance to a shopping mall, you may use your hand to trace an archway in the air.

We also sometimes use gestures without any words, like shrugging, waving, holding up an index finger to say "just a minute," or putting an index finger to our lips to say "be quiet."

Avoid pointing at people or putting a hand up toward someone's face while they are talking, as these gestures can make some people feel attacked. Sticking out the middle finger might seem like a funny joke to some, but it could be offensive to others.

When you're not sure how someone will respond to a gesture, don't use it at all.

Touch

How comfortable people are with being touched varies a lot between different cultures, which can be important to consider if you are interacting with someone from a different background. Comfort with touch also varies depending on what's going on in the world; for example, when a contagious illness is surging, most people avoid physical contact to prevent germs from spreading. The more familiar we are with someone, like a family member, best friend, or romantic partner, the more appropriate it is to touch that person. But even loved ones should respect your personal boundaries regarding touch.

Sometimes good friends hug when they see each other for the first time in a while or say goodbye, unless there are health risks involved with physical contact. There are also subtler forms of touch, like gently putting your hand on someone's shoulder or arm to indicate that the conversation is important or that you are paying special attention to what they are saying. Someone may also do this to show affection.

However, not everyone is comfortable being touched even in a casual way, and such touch can be misinterpreted as being too forward or even flirtatious in certain situations. It's always okay to tell someone that you are not comfortable being touched. Many individuals with sensory sensitivities may even find physical touch unpleasant. A small tap on the back, for example, may feel very uncomfortable. It's important to communicate your boundaries to others.

Generally, hold off on any kind of touch with someone you don't know well.

Tone and Volume

In addition to words and nonverbal ways of communicating, you can use your tone of voice to convey your feelings and mood. Your **pitch** and **tone** of voice refer to the way that your voice rises and falls when you talk.

When someone uses a frustrated tone, their words might sound more forceful, getting louder at the end of the sentence. When we hear this type of tone, we are likely to respond in a defensive manner, which can even lead to an argument. A gentler tone might be conveyed by someone's voice rising in pitch a bit at the end of the sentence. This usually reflects openness.

Your volume also affects the quality of your communication. Generally, it's a good idea to match the volume of other people's voices. You don't want your voice to soar above everyone else's or be too quiet for others to hear. If you are not sure how to gauge your own volume, pay attention to people's nonverbal responses for cues. If someone frowns, backs up, or leans away when you speak, you might want to adjust the volume of your voice.

Humor

We use humor to relate to other people. We also use it to defuse awkward, tense, or otherwise uncomfortable situations. It can come in the form of jokes, witty remarks, or observations that others also find funny. Sharing a similar sense of humor helps us connect.

For example, imagine you're eating lunch with a friend in the cafeteria; he opens a can of soda, and it sprays in his face. You both laugh at the unexpected and sudden shower that he just received. This experience can put you both at ease and give you something to talk about. It can even create a memory you can look back on.

But you also have to watch your friend's reaction carefully. Though he laughed at first, he may soon feel uncomfortable about being wet, or embarrassed that others saw. If he stops laughing, you might want to stop laughing, too. If you don't, he might think you're no longer laughing *with* him, but *at* him. Though it's fun to laugh with someone over a shared experience, most people don't like feeling that someone is laughing at them.

An **inside joke** is something that just a few people know about, and other people probably do not know about. Inside jokes can be a great way for a group of peers to connect over mutual stories, funny memories, or observations that make people laugh.

However, make sure that the jokes don't go too far. A joke may unintentionally offend people if they take it personally, or if there's truth to the joke that hurts their feelings. Sometimes a joke starts to lose its humor if repeated too many times.

Be more careful about using humor when you meet people for the first time.

Personal Space

Your personal space refers to the physical space around your body, kind of like an imaginary bubble that surrounds you when you are interacting with someone. If you stand too close to another person, you may pop the bubble, which means you're invading someone else's personal space. When you do so, they will feel uncomfortable, making it hard for them to focus on the actual conversation or interaction.

The goal is to be close enough that the other person knows you are talking to them and can hear you, but not so close that the person feels uncomfortable. Usually this means standing 1.5 to 3 feet (about an arm's length) away from the other person. Sometimes, for instance, if one of you is sick, it is healthier to stand even farther away (at least 6 feet) to prevent the spread of germs. Make even more space when interacting with someone less familiar, such as an acquaintance.

Like with other types of body language, look for cues from the other person and mirror their use of personal space. If someone takes a small step closer, that could be a sign that they're eager to interact. If you are comfortable with the amount of space, you may also take a small step forward to reciprocate. Similarly, if someone leans back or backs away from you, it might signal that the other person needs more space.

STRANGER	FRIEND	FAMILY/INTIMATE

These strategies can work for you, too. To show that you need a bigger bubble, start by leaning back, pushing your chair a few inches away, or taking a small step backward. The other person should start to mirror your actions by giving you some space. If not, it's okay to tell them that you need a little more space and perhaps even explain why you are not comfortable being so close. You could say, "Would you mind stepping back just a little? I would be more comfortable if I had more space."

Having Conversations

In an informal conversation, two or more people chat, usually without any expectation of what they should be talking about. Most social conversations tend to be informal. The main purpose of a conversation is not to explain something or prove a point, but to exchange ideas and thoughts.

By exchanging ideas, you get to know each other better. Asking about the other person shows that you *want* to get to know them. When you ask questions, it shows that you value their point of view.

Conversation tends to *flow* better when you have a common interest that you can talk about, so you want to make sure the other person has an interest in the topic as well. To determine whether the other person shares your interest, use nonverbal cues to help decide how motivated the other person seems. Ask yourself if they are facing and looking at you. Look for other signals like whether they're nodding their head, smiling, or asking you follow-up questions that show they are enjoying the conversation.

Meeting for the First Time

If you're meeting someone for the first time, use a more formal greeting. For example, imagine your basketball teammate introducing you to his brother after practice. You can wait for his brother's nonverbal cue to help decide how to greet him. For example, does he reach his hand out to shake your hand? Does he say hello from a distance and nod with a smile? Follow the other person's cues and mirror their greeting style. Never force physical contact (like a handshake or hug) on someone.

Acknowledge the person by looking at them while smiling, say something like, "Nice to meet you," and tell them your name. If you are all rushing to leave practice, that might be the end of the greeting. However, if you have a moment, you can follow the greeting with a question relevant to the situation. For example, you can ask, "Do you play basketball, too?" or, "Are you in town visiting?" Avoid asking personal questions like, "Is that your girlfriend?" about a friend he brought with him, or, "Nice shoes—how much did you pay for those?" even if you feel like you "know" him because you have a mutual friend.

Greeting Someone You Know

To greet someone you've met before but don't know well, you can use a phrase like, "What's up?" or, "Good to see you." Sometimes we even ask, "How are you?" If you're walking past someone on your way to class, you can ask, "How are you?" as a sign of acknowledgment and interest, but you don't have to expect the other person to answer the question literally by elaborating on how they're feeling.

On the other hand, if you are standing or sitting with someone already and they ask, "How are you?" this might be an opportunity to tell them something about your day and to ask them the same question.

Remember that every interaction is different depending on the situation. Even best friends or close family can sometimes be too busy to talk or even say hi. That doesn't have to mean anything bad about your relationship.

Formal versus Informal

Once you and the other person have started talking, monitor your conversation depending on whom you are talking to.

If you run into a teacher at a grocery store, for example, your conversation may be more formal than if you were at home with your best friend. When a conversation is more formal, avoid getting too serious or personal. You might ask your teacher how their day is going or if they like shopping at that store—questions that you believe they would be comfortable answering. This is probably not the time to share too much personal information, like an argument you just had with your parents or the upset stomach that you had that morning. If the teacher asks about your family or what you're up to that weekend, it's perfectly fine to answer those questions if you feel comfortable.

Chatting with your best friend at home, on the other hand, is informal. You might joke around or talk about personal topics including stress, big decisions you're grappling with, or exciting news you want to share. You might even bring up something funny that happened in the past if it has become an inside joke.

Starting a Conversation

Once you've greeted someone and decided whether it's a formal or informal interaction, consider if it's the right time to start a conversation. Here are some tips for starting a conversation and keeping it going.

Finding the Right Time

Before starting a conversation, make sure that the circumstances are right. Here's a list of questions to ask yourself:

- Is it a good time to talk?
- Are you two rushing in different directions?
- Is it too loud and crowded?
- If it *is* loud and crowded, can you move to a better place to have a conversation?
- Is the person giving nonverbal clues that show they're interested in talking (like looking at you, facing your direction, or slowing down to walk with you)?

For example, imagine you have a few minutes between classes, and you see a friend. You want to ask her about her weekend plans. First, take a moment to assess the situation. If your friend is reviewing notes because she has an exam soon or if she's rushing to get to her classroom, now might not be the best time to talk. In that situation, it might be best to smile, wave, and save any question that requires a response for a time when she is less occupied.

Choosing a Topic

To start a conversation, people generally make a comment, ask a direct question, or give a compliment. If you are less familiar with a person, make a more general comment or ask a question about the situation. For example, you might talk about where you both happen to be standing or about the weather—something you're both experiencing at that moment.

If you are more familiar with the person, you can ask a question that is more personally relevant, like how they're doing that day. Giving someone a compliment on their new shoes or phone can also be a good conversation starter.

If you run into someone you've met once or twice before, keep the conversation brief and casual. Start by talking about something you're experiencing together. For example, if you're new to a school and it's lunchtime, you might want to chat with a student who is trying to decide what to get for lunch. You may ask whether the same food options are served every day or if desserts are offered. If the student answers the question, you can make a comment or ask a follow-up question, continuing the conversation.

If you meet someone or are introduced to someone for the first time, show that you are happy to meet them and interested in getting to know them by asking some basic questions about them, like how they know your mutual friends (if you were introduced), whether they live nearby, and whether they've been to the place where you are meeting before.

Depending on the situation and how familiar we are with a person, there are a number of ways to start a conversation. What are some ways to start a conversation in the following situations?

- You're in line with a friend at the school cafeteria.
- You run into your soccer coach at a local restaurant.
- You're waiting to be picked up from school, and you see a kid you recognize from one of your classes, but you have forgotten his name.
- You notice that your classmate's new backpack is the same as yours.
- You admire your neighbor's new scooter as she's riding it outside.
- You're sitting at a table in the cafeteria with a couple of other kids and a squirrel jumps onto the table, trying to eat everyone's food.

Share your answers with your family or trusted friends to see what they think.

Taking Turns

A conversation should go back and forth between you and other people. Be aware of how much you are talking to make sure you are not taking too many turns. To keep a conversation reciprocal, try the following:

- After you say something, pause and give the other person a chance to ask a question or add a comment.
- Ask open-ended questions that give the other person the opportunity to elaborate. Open-ended questions like, "What have you been up to lately?" or, "How's your day going?" don't have yes/no answers.
- Try not to interview the other person with too many yes/no questions. This could make the other person feel uncomfortable. Make sure to give the other person the chance to ask you questions in return.
- Give one or two details with your answers instead of one-word responses.

Look for ways to build on the conversation. For example, if your friend asks you if you have plans for the weekend and you simply answer, "Yes," your friend has to work very hard to keep the conversation going. They may have to ask numerous follow-up questions like, "What are your plans?" and, "Whom are you going with?"

Instead, make your answer descriptive, like, "Yes, I am seeing the new Star Wars movie," and follow up with a question like, "Have you seen it yet?" By providing an interesting detail and following up with a question, you are showing your friend that you want to share information and keep the conversation going.

Active Listening

Even though it might not seem like it, listening is a very active process. In addition to taking in the information and making sense of it, you need to *show* the other person that you are listening. By listening attentively, you are showing that you value what they are saying.

To show that you are listening, try the following:

- Check in with eye contact.
- Nod from time to time.
- Respond briefly using, "Mm-hmm," "Uh-huh," "Gotcha," "That's cool," or, "Really?"
- Ask a question about what the other person just said.
- Reflect back your friend's feelings. For example, if your friend tells you about something good that happened, you can say something like, "Nice! You must have been so excited."
- Ask questions about things you don't understand or that you want to learn more about.

Listening also means waiting to share thoughts or opinions. When there is a pause in the conversation, ask a specific question about something that your friend said, or share a similar experience to show that you understand.

Active Listening Posture

Barely Listening Posture

You can even ask for clarification if your friend was talking too fast or using terms you don't know. Asking for clarification or asking someone to explain something in a different way is another way of showing interest.

Ending a Conversation

When it's time to end the conversation, give the other person some warning so that the conversation doesn't end abruptly. Try the following steps:

- Wait for a pause in the conversation.
- During the pause, give a brief reason for ending the conversation.
- Say something polite about the conversation.
- Turn your body away and say goodbye.

For example, let's say you run into your neighbor outside and you have a brief conversation about school. To end the conversation, wait for a brief pause, and then tell the neighbor, "I've got to head back in to work on my homework," or, "I should run inside since my mom just got home." It's good to be specific, but you don't need to give too much detail.

As you turn to leave, you may want to make a polite and positive comment to show that you enjoyed the conversation. For example, you can say, "It was great running into you," "See you again soon," or, "It was nice chatting with you!" Then wave (while making eye contact) and say goodbye as you walk away.

SENSITIVE TOPICS TO AVOID

There are certain topics people generally try to avoid during conversation because they can stir up strong feelings or reactions. Here are some examples of sensitive topics to avoid with people you don't know very well:

- Body image ("Are you trying to lose weight?"; "What size pants do you wear?"; "You're so skinny!")
- Physical appearance ("You're so short!"; "Didn't you wear that shirt yesterday?")
- Eating habits ("I can't believe you eat that!"; "You eat like a bird; are you on a diet?"; "Your food is smelly.")
- Religion ("You don't celebrate Christmas? Why not?"; "Do you go to church?")
- Politics ("Whom did your parents vote for?"; "Do you support abortion?")
- Money ("Your house is awesome! Do your parents make a lot of money?"; "How much did that cost?")

Typically, these topics are reserved for talk within a family or with a close friend, when we have knowledge of the person's background and a sense of what could potentially be perceived as offensive.

▶ REFLECTION QUESTIONS

- How could you start a conversation with someone in your class who you want to get to know better?
- How do you feel now about greeting someone you don't know very well? Do you feel more prepared to engage in conversations with other people?
- What is your favorite way to communicate with other people: verbal, nonverbal, written, online, or some other way?

CHAPTER THREE

OTHER CODES OF BEHAVIOR

When it comes to social interactions, you might feel like there is a secret code that everyone seems to know but you don't. For example, there are unspoken rules about how people should behave in a doctor's office, at the beach, or at a restaurant. Not knowing them can make for awkward social interactions. These informal rules are not typically written down (though there are books about manners), and no one can punish you by law if you don't follow them. But it helps to know what other people expect from you in certain situations. In this chapter, we'll review some common social etiquette guidelines and how they affect everyday communication.

- Do you sometimes have a hard time figuring out what someone *really* means when they say something, as if there are hidden messages behind their words?
- Do you have a hard time figuring out if someone is being sarcastic or if they are being serious?
- How can you tell someone's tone during an online conversation? What clues can you look for?

When People Don't Say What They Mean

Life would be so much easier if people just said exactly what they meant! In fact, this may seem so obvious to most teens on the spectrum. You may be the kind of person who is pretty direct and says exactly what you mean. Why would you say something when you don't actually mean it?

However, there are a number of reasons why someone may not always say what they mean, depending on the context. People try to be polite or spare someone's feelings, especially when they're not sure how the other person will respond. Other times, someone may even try to indirectly insult you, such as by saying, "Cute shoes," in a sarcastic tone that suggests they are actually mocking you for the shoes you're wearing.

It can be difficult to know when someone means something different than what they say, but you can look for cues in the tone of their voice, an emphasis on a word, or a change in facial expression. For example, you notice your mom sighing and muttering under her breath. You ask, "Are you okay?" and she looks away, furrows her eyebrows, and answers, "I'm *fine.*" The word *fine* is spoken with emphasis and louder than the word *I'm.* She said she was fine, but you have clues from her behavior and facial expression, as well as tone of her voice, that she is actually quite frustrated. In this example, you have to take in the cues other than her words to really know the meaning of what she says.

Let's take another example of how the *way* someone says something changes the meaning. Let's say you and your sister are opening presents for a big holiday. You say, "I can't wait to see what Audrey gets." Now, when you say the sentence out loud, try emphasizing different words in the sentence to see how doing so changes the meaning. First, try, "I can't *wait* to see what Audrey gets." Then say, "I can't wait to see what *Audrey* gets!" Finally, say, "I can't wait to see what Audrey *gets!*"

Now, imagine that you say that first sentence with an eye roll: "I can't *wait* to see what Audrey gets." What kind of meaning does that sentence have now? It sounds a bit sarcastic or like you might be annoyed even thinking about your sister getting a present. For the second example, imagine that you smile and look in your sister's direction when you say, "I can't wait to see what *Audrey* gets!" This sounds like you're excited for your sister and you really can't wait to see what she gets; is it different from the present *you* got? And, finally, imagine you are smiling with your eyes wide open while your sister opens her present, and you exclaim, "I can't wait to see what Audrey *gets!*" You seem very focused on the gift itself ... what could it be?

Here are some common examples of when we say one thing but mean something a little different.

Rhetorical Questions

"How are you?" is a common way to greet someone. It's so common that we hear it in numerous contexts, ranging from the cashier at the grocery checkout to your best friend who you talk to at the end of a school day.

In many contexts, especially when the encounter is brief (like at the grocery store) or the greeting is in passing (like walking past someone in the hallway at school), "How are you?" is a friendly way of saying hello. It is often a **rhetorical question**, which means it does not require a full response other than something general like, "Good, thanks," or, "Good, how are you?" Because autistic people may have a tendency to take things more literally than others, it's good to know that you don't always have to respond to rhetorical questions.

When someone is expressing disbelief or surprise, they may make a comment like, "Are you serious?", "Seriously?", or, "Are you kidding me?" You don't have to stop your story to address whether you are serious about what happened. This rhetorical comment is just a way for your friend to show that they understand it's a big deal. You can respond by saying something like, "I know, right?"

We sometimes make self-deprecating comments when we're frustrated with ourselves. You might be shooting hoops with someone when they exclaim, "Ugh, what is my problem?" or, "What's wrong with me?" You don't need to explain what the problem might actually be. You could simply give a brief statement of encouragement to show that you understand that your friend is frustrated, like, "Shooting from that angle is tough."

Even if the rhetorical question is directed toward you—like if you poke a little fun at your friend and they ask, "You think you're so funny, huh?"—this is their way of calling you out for trying to be funny. You don't have to defend yourself or answer their question. You can simply smile in response.

White Lies

A white lie is a small or trivial lie that is sometimes used in order to avoid hurting someone's feelings. For example, imagine you are at your friend's house for dinner, and your friend's mom baked a pie for dessert. She asks if you like it. It's not your favorite, and you like your mom's pie better. But to be polite and spare her feelings, you state, "Yes, it's great!" Although it's important to be honest, being *too* direct and honest can sometimes hurt people's feelings. In this example, if you said, "My mom makes a way better pie," you could come across as rude and hurtful.

When someone asks your opinion about their cooking, artwork, clothing, hair, or another characteristic, be careful about offending them. Imagine a friend asking, "Do you like my haircut?" They obviously can't undo the haircut, and you don't want to hurt their feelings, but what if you thought it looked better before? It's okay to say, "It's different!" and try to say something you like about it, such as, "I like the new bangs!" If you simply say, "It was better before," your friend's feelings might be hurt.

Although white lies are common, the best plan is usually to tell the truth in a gentle way. In the example about eating pie at your friend's house, you can be truthful without being insulting. For example, you can say, "I'm used to my mom's pie, which is my favorite. But this is good. I'm happy I tried a new one!"

When explaining something about your behavior, consider whether a white lie will start to become an actual lie. For example, if you were late to meet someone, it's probably best to just tell the truth. Telling your friend the truth—"Sorry, I couldn't find my bag, so it took me forever to get out the door"—is probably just as effective as a white lie like, "Sorry, my mom made me late." Honesty is usually a good policy. Imagine if, when your mom came to pick you up, your friend jokingly said, "Good thing you're not late this time!" Your mom might look confused. Your friend might then realize you had lied about why you were late when you first arrived. In addition to creating an awkward situation, you run the risk of seeming dishonest.

White lies can be told about opinions, like how much you like a pie or a haircut. But they should not be told about facts, like what grade you're in, what make of car you have, or what score you got on your SATs. At that point, you're not telling a white lie to spare someone else's feelings—you're telling a self-serving lie to make yourself seem more interesting or important.

Other people may be telling you white lies, too, to spare your feelings. For example, if you ask someone, "Do you like this shirt on me?" and they hesitate and then say, "Yeah . . . it's cute," they might not be sure how they feel about it or might not like it. It's okay to clarify. You can ask, "Are you just saying that so you don't hurt my feelings? It's okay to tell me." But if you ask someone for the truth, be prepared—you might not like what they have to say!

Making Sense of Figurative Language

Figurative language is when we use words in an unusual or imaginative way. The words or phrasing of the words go beyond the normal, everyday, literal meaning to convey a certain message. We use figurative language to make things sound more dramatic or interesting or to provide someone with a colorful image when we are telling a story.

Idioms

An idiom is a common word or phrase that is known within a culture to mean something other than what the specific words might suggest. The meaning of the phrase cannot be determined by the literal meaning of the individual words.

For example, "It's raining cats and dogs," does not literally mean that cats and dogs are falling from the sky. Rather, individuals familiar with English understand that this term means that it is raining really hard. Another common example is, "Let's hit the road." If we were to interpret the individual words of the phrase literally, it might mean to physically punch the road rather than, "Let's go," or, "It's time to leave."

Idioms can be an interesting way to express yourself. They're also a way to show other people that you share a common language with them. It's fun to see how idioms and expressions differ depending on where you grew up.

In the Resources section, I list a helpful book on common idioms and expressions. Learning about them can help you feel more prepared when talking to other people. You might even pick up some favorite idioms yourself.

Irony and Sarcasm

When someone is being ironic, they say something that is the opposite of what they mean, usually to be funny. For example, when a student finds out that the teacher assigned another exam, they might say, "Oh good, I just *love* taking tests." This is, of course, the opposite of what they really mean. They might even emphasize the word *love* because that word represents the opposite meaning.

In another example, imagine your friend broke her leg and has been stuck at home for a couple of weeks. You go to visit her, and you feel a little nervous seeing her; you wonder if she will be really upset about her leg and missing out on so much. When you ask what she's been up to, she smiles and says, "Oh you know, just *dancing* around and having the best time!" Once she says this, you see that she is joking and making light of the situation, which puts you both at ease.

Using irony in this way can lighten a mood or defuse a stressful situation. For example, if everyone is stressing out about having to prep for another test, the student's comment about "loving" tests may make everyone laugh and reduce the tension. It can add humor to an otherwise stressful situation.

Sarcasm uses irony to make fun of something. It's typically associated with being humorous or witty but can sometimes be used to insult someone. Deciphering when someone is being sarcastic can be challenging because their tone might sound normal or only change subtly. Usually sarcasm has a negative or matter-of-fact tone.

For example, your mom asks you to take the garbage out, and you answer, "I'd love to." Of course, you probably don't really love taking the trash out, so your response is sarcastic. Though this is similar to being ironic, the slight bitterness or negativity in your matter-of-fact tone can be interpreted as being insulting or disrespectful. Maybe you even roll your eyes as you make the comment.

Teens use sarcasm a lot. It's often a form of humor, and like irony, it can defuse tension. If your friend squirts mustard all over his shirt and you say, "Nice. Looks like you're trying to match the restaurant decor," the sarcastic joke could make your friend feel more comfortable rather than embarrassed. Sarcasm also helps you bond with people because it can let you connect over a shared feeling or add humor to a situation.

While sarcasm can be funny, be careful not to use it too much. There is a fine line between sarcastic humor and being mean. For example, if someone hits a tennis ball into the net and you say, "Nice shot," sarcastically, that would come off as mean. If your friend fails their exam, avoid using sarcastic comments like, "You must have stayed up late studying!"—that might make them feel worse.

Exaggeration

Hyperbole or exaggeration in speech is another type of figurative language. It's used to get a point across when you really want to emphasize something. For example, you might say, "My backpack weighs 500 pounds," to emphasize that it's *really* heavy. Or you might tell your friend, "My sister takes 10 hours to get ready in the morning," or, "My neighbor has a hundred cats in her yard."

Sometimes, these exaggerations can be humorous and give you a vivid picture when you visualize them. They also help convince the person of just how extreme (big, heavy, time-consuming) something might be.

While hyperboles are common and can definitely help emphasize your point, they can also come across as a bit dramatic or even as a complaint. Your backpack might be heavy, for example, but is it actually that heavy? Don't exaggerate too much, or people might think you are *always* exaggerating. Next time you mention that your backpack is heavier than your little sister, people might not take you seriously!

Slang

Slang is another type of informal use of words or phrases that have a specific meaning for a culture. Like idioms, they don't really mean what the words would suggest. But they are different from idioms because only a subset of the culture understands what they mean, and their significance changes relatively quickly. For example, teens often use slang that their parents don't understand. Your parents probably used their own slang when they were younger.

A number of examples of current slang like *lit* and *sick* describe something exciting or cool. But by the time you're reading this book, those might be hopelessly out of date! If someone uses slang and you don't know what it means, it's okay to ask or look it up online.

In the following scenarios, try to determine whether the statement or question in **bold** is sarcastic. If someone is saying the *opposite* of what is actually happening, chances are they are being sarcastic.

1. English class just started, and your teacher starts handing out exams. A few minutes later, one of your classmates slides into his seat, and you hear his friend say, **"Well, aren't *you* punctual?"**

2. You're driving with your mom right after she got her car washed. A bird poops all over the windshield. She shakes her head and says, **"Perfect!"**

3. You're driving with your mom, and she spots a parking spot right in front of the store you are going to. She smiles and says, **"Perfect!"**

4. Your dad reminds you that you have a class party at school the next day, and you've been looking forward to it. You reply, **"Sweet, I can't *wait!*"**

5. Your dad reminds you that you promised to spend all day Saturday cleaning out the garage with him. You mumble, **"Sweet, I can't wait."**

6. Your friend runs into class sopping wet from the rain. You ask, **"Nice weather out there?"**

Answers:

1. Sarcastic
2. Sarcastic
3. Not sarcastic
4. Not sarcastic
5. Sarcastic
6. Sarcastic

Online Etiquette

When you text or email, there's no pressure to think about body language, facial expression, and other nonverbal communication. Because you can focus more on the words themselves, online exchanges can feel much easier than real-life conversation.

But without nonverbal cues, you have to pay extra attention to the context online. For example, is your friend in a good mood when they get your text? Or are they busy and distracted? You won't always have these answers, making it difficult to interpret their words.

Remember that when you are texting or emailing, no one knows if you are smiling, joking around, or using a serious tone. All of this has to be conveyed through your typed messages. You might think you are sending a funny text and unintentionally offend the other person.

Before sending a message, always ask yourself if you would say the same thing to the person face-to-face. You may feel protected behind the screen and free from the consequences of your actions, but your words and pictures can still have a big impact on the other person.

Remember that anything that you write on text, email, or social media is permanent. Anyone can take a screenshot of your message or picture and send it to another person you wouldn't want to share it with. Even if you delete it on your phone or computer, it may exist on someone else's. Before sending a message or picture, always consider how you would feel if your message or picture was sent to someone else.

Texting

Since texting is casual, we typically don't text with teachers or people in a professional role unless they text us first. Text messages are typically short. Save longer, more in-depth discussions for a phone call or email. This is especially true if you expect the conversation might affect the reader in a significant way, like sharing sad news.

Because you can't share nonverbal information with the person you're texting, make your text messages extra clear. For example, if you are making plans to meet someone, be specific about the time and place. It's also important that your texts are not too vague or lacking punctuation that can change the meaning of the message.

Because text messages *are* a casual medium, many people will leave out punctuation, drop words, or misspell things, which can lead to misunderstandings. If you don't understand a text you've received, request clarification. Here are some examples of how text messages can be misinterpreted:

UNCLEAR TEXT MESSAGE	POSSIBLE INTERPRETATIONS	BETTER TEXT MESSAGE
"Call me"	"Call me right away; something important has happened!" *or* "It would be nice to talk on the phone whenever you're available."	"Give me a call later if you get the chance"
"Where r u"	"I'm angry because you're late" *or* "I'm worried that I can't find you" *or* "Am I waiting for you in the wrong place?"	"We're supposed to meet at the Starbucks on Main St, right? I'm here but I don't see you"
"Can't"	"I can't do the thing you just asked me to do, and I'm angry that you'd even ask" *or* "I can't do that exact thing at this exact moment in time, but it's nothing personal."	"I can't tonight but let's plan something for tomorrow!"

People tend to use lots of abbreviations when texting, like "lol" for "laughing out loud," "brb" for "be right back," "jk" for "just kidding," "ty" for "thank you," and "np" for "no problem." Make sure to clarify if you're not sure about an abbreviation. Only use an abbreviation if you're sure of the meaning. If you're not sure if someone else uses the same abbreviations as you, write out the whole word to make sure your meaning is clear.

People often respond to text messages quickly, but you never know if someone is doing something that prevents them from responding right away. Even if you are eager for a response, try to be patient and wait for the other person to reply. While you wait, try putting your phone away, or play a game on your phone to keep yourself busy. Texting again and again hoping to speed up the person's response could actually be misinterpreted as being annoying, intrusive, or even aggressive. When someone texts multiple times in a row without waiting for a response, it is called *spamming*.

This is particularly true when it comes to friendships and dating. Texting relentlessly without a response could be perceived as being pushy and make someone feel uncomfortable. Similarly, when someone writes something that indicates they are ending the text conversation, like, "Have a good night," respond in the same way and then stop texting until at least the next day.

Too many emojis and gifs can be distracting, so generally use them only when necessary to clarify or emphasize how you feel or what you mean—unless you have the sort of texting relationship with somebody where you both like to send a lot of gifs!

Email

Email is more formal than texting. In emails, we tend to compose longer messages, using complete sentences and fewer casual abbreviations than we would in a text message. Since emails tend to be longer than texts, many people wait until they are at a computer or have a quiet moment in the day to respond. Typically, people respond to emails within one or two days, but, as with texts, a delayed reply might just mean that they're busy and not that they're ignoring the sender.

Email is a great way to communicate with teachers, supervisors, and other people who are in professional roles. For example, if you volunteer at a church or school, you would probably email with staff members to coordinate your schedule. You may also email with friends and family members, especially if you are conveying a lot of information or want to communicate to a group of people all at once.

One of the benefits of email is that you can take the time to reread or proofread your messages before you send them. This is especially important if you are emailing a group of people and you want to consider how each person will interpret your message.

Be careful about "replying all" to a group email if your response applies to only one or a few people in the group. If you reply all, you might accidentally share information with multiple people that you meant only for one person. It can also annoy everyone on the email chain to get replies going back and forth that aren't relevant to them.

Put a heading in the subject line of your email that shows the purpose of the email to let the person receiving it know what the email is about and why they should open it. Doing so also makes it easier for you to search for the email in your inbox later. At the end of your email, add a closing statement like "Sincerely," "Best," or "Thanks," and your name below it.

Because emails are typically more formal than text messages, avoid using too many emojis or exclamation points, which can come across as immature or unprofessional. Also be cautious when using humor, since the tone of your words can get lost over email. Keep in mind that emails can be forwarded to others, so you don't want to share anything too private or controversial.

Social Media

Social media is a wonderful way to connect with others and build an online community. It helps us keep in touch with old friends and distant family members, and connect with new people all over the world. But there are a few important guidelines to keep in mind when considering how to use social media.

MANAGING YOUR ONLINE PERSONA

Keep in mind that there is a record of everything you post online. When it comes time to apply for a job or when you make a new friend, people can look up your name and see everything you've posted online. Because of this, be thoughtful about posting personal information and pictures, or anything that could be interpreted as controversial or inappropriate.

To know if something is controversial or inappropriate, you can first run it by a parent or trusted friend to see how your post could be interpreted before posting. You can also sleep on it and wait until the next day before deciding to post. Ask yourself if there is any chance you would regret the post later or your post could hurt someone else. Ask yourself how you would feel if someone took a screenshot of your post and showed it to their parents or teachers. If you are unsure, it's best to not post.

When you comment on someone else's picture, followers of that person also see your comment. This can include people you've never met. Before commenting, think carefully about whether you want your comment to be visible to everyone. Even though you might be able to delete a comment or post after changing your mind, it might be too late if people have read it or saved it as a screenshot.

To make sure that your account is private, double-check the settings. On most social media networks like Facebook and Instagram, you can go to Settings and find the Privacy page. Make sure to keep your account "Private" so that only friends or followers can view your pictures, posts, and comments. Regularly check these settings.

REACTING TO DIFFERENT OPINIONS

Certain posts or comments might trigger your feelings in some way. Even if you have a strong reaction to something, be careful not to be reactive. Save the serious debates for face-to-face interactions where you're not leaving a permanent record of your thoughts.

The problem with leaving a permanent record is that your ideas and opinions may change one day, and you may regret that there is a public record of your thoughts. You might also offend someone without meaning to, and that person might show your post to others. For example, if you make a comment that is misinterpreted as bullying, racist, sexist, threatening, or offensive in some other way, a student could take a screenshot and show it to the school principal. There is little tolerance at schools and other places for inappropriate statements, and you don't want to be in the position of having to defend something you posted.

If you have strong feelings about a topic, be careful about how you express your beliefs online since anyone can challenge your opinions in a very public way. This can lead to online arguments with people criticizing you or making hurtful comments. Because of the nature of the internet, anything controversial could get a lot of attention, creating more conflict. In general, keep these discussions offline.

It's also best not to communicate while you or the other person is emotional. Avoid posting online when you are feeling really angry or frustrated. Talk it through with someone else and try to calm down first.

OVERSHARING

While it is nice to post an occasional picture or update on social media, be careful not to over-post. People generally like occasional posts about big accomplishments or important events. But how do you feel when other people post every single thing about their lives down to the most mundane events of the day, like what they had for breakfast, how well they slept, or what they bought at the grocery store? Too many posts begin to feel a bit redundant and self-absorbed.

Here are some questions you can ask yourself before sharing something online:

- Is there a chance you would change your mind about this post in a few days?
- Would your post seem gross or disturbing to some people, even if you find it funny?
- Would you show this post to your parents or teachers?
- How would you feel if someone at school asked you about your post?

PERSONAL INFORMATION

When sharing information about yourself or other people, first determine how personal that information is. For example, overly personal information could make others feel uncomfortable. Protecting personal information is particularly important online, since others can misinterpret your message or even misuse the information for their benefit.

Here are some personal details you should keep private:

- Social security number
- Phone number
- Home address, unless you're on a trusted website
- Bathroom experiences
- Information about bodily changes (like during puberty)
- Medical information
- Details about arguments you've had with others
- Family conflicts that your parents or other people may be going through
- Your family's finances, like how much money your parents make or how much they paid for something

If you are very close to someone, like a best friend, you may choose to share this type of information in person and discuss other sensitive topics. If you're not sure whether it's okay to bring up something personal in person, wait to see if the other person brings up a sensitive topic or asks you a personal question before deciding how much you feel okay sharing.

- Can you think of a time when you've told a white lie and you shouldn't have? What about a time when you were overly direct and should have told a white lie instead?
- Can you think of a time when you and a friend had a miscommunication over text? What went wrong, and what can you do to prevent that in the future?
- Have you ever posted something online and then regretted it later? How did you handle it? Is there anything you would do differently after reading this chapter?

PART TWO
· · · · · · · · · · · · · · · · ·

TAKING CARE
OF YOURSELF

Taking care of yourself means checking in with your own body and emotional reactions on a regular basis. Understanding what triggers you and how you react in different situations can help you learn more about yourself and feel more prepared for those scenarios in the future. In part 2, you'll learn strategies for checking in with yourself, how to handle strong impulses in different situations, and tips for managing your feelings. Your thoughts and feelings matter. Paying careful attention to them can help you feel more in control and confident when interacting with other people.

CHAPTER FOUR

YOUR EMOTIONS

Emotions are automatic reactions you experience when you see, hear, or even think of something. When you feel an emotion, your body reacts in certain ways. These physical responses, like an increased heart rate, are clues to help identify and understand your own feelings. When you learn to identify your own feelings, you can communicate them to others more easily. And when you can identify other people's feelings, it becomes that much easier to empathize with them and strengthen relationships.

In this chapter, we'll explore what emotions are and review the basic human emotions. You'll also get tips for identifying and understanding feelings, whether your own or other people's, so you can feel more comfortable expressing yourself and feel more connected to the people who matter to you.

- How does your body signal that you're angry, sad, or anxious?
- What are some situations that tend to trigger strong feelings in you?
- What are some strategies you've been using to detect emotions in others?

What Emotions Feel Like

Emotions, like anger, disgust, fear, happiness, sadness, and surprise, are connected to physical sensations in our bodies. Sometimes we notice these bodily reactions before we even have a name for the feeling we have.

Your body gives you clues to help you identify your emotions. For example, imagine sitting in class and waiting your turn for your oral presentation. When your name is called, you might feel your heart beating faster than usual, or you might feel hot. You may even notice that your hands are trembling. That's your body's way of communicating that you're nervous.

As you become more aware of your bodily cues, you get better at naming your emotions. This helps you communicate your feelings with friends more easily and react to them appropriately.

The physical sensations that go with each emotion may differ from person to person, but here are a few examples of common reactions that people experience.

Fear

When you are scared, your brain tells your body to prepare for **fight or flight**. Imagine being faced with a tiger, and in order to survive, you have to either fight the tiger or run! In either case, your heart beats faster, you breathe faster, and your body tenses up. When you feel stressed or anxious, your body may respond like this, even when you aren't facing a real tiger. Whenever your brain *thinks* you are in danger, it prepares your body for fight or flight. You may have experienced a situation that provoked anxiety and made you want to escape right away; this is your body wanting to flee.

A **stressor** is something that causes you to have a stressful or anxious response. Certain stressors may be more specific to autistic people who have sensory differences. For example, in a classroom full of other students, you might be overcome by different smells as your peers walk by your desk. You may hear every pencil scraping paper, the clock ticking, or the buzzing of the fluorescent lights. These stressors can be so overstimulating that they make it difficult to focus on schoolwork or on class discussions. This type of stress can lead to a similar fear response in your body, which can be very unpleasant to experience day after day.

Anxiety and Anger

When you're anxious, your brain sends messages to the rest of your body to gear up. It activates your lungs, heart, and muscles to get you ready for potential danger. You may feel your heart racing, your muscles tense, and the palms of your hands get sweaty. Some people also feel slightly dizzy or feel their stomach tighten or ache.

These physical sensations can be overwhelming. For example, if you feel anxiety for a prolonged period of time, your muscles can get tired of being tense, and you might even feel aches and pains. In fact, many people go to the doctor due to headaches, stomachaches, or neck and shoulder pain without realizing their symptoms could be related to anxiety.

Like fear and anxiety, anger is also related to the fight-or-flight response. When you feel angry, your heart beats faster, your muscles tense (especially in your jaw), and your body starts to sweat. Your body becomes activated and energized by the effects of adrenaline as it fuels your muscles with the oxygen needed to fight. Your body may feel hot, especially in your chest, neck, and face.

Happiness and Sadness

For some people, being happy can make them feel content and relaxed as the heart rate slows down. But happiness can also make people want to jump for joy or activate their bodies so that they feel excited. Happiness can be associated with a lot of different situations, from sitting on a beach to flying through the air on a roller coaster. Depending on the circumstances, the body reacts in different ways.

Feeling sad or down can slow down the body. You might feel like it takes a lot more effort than usual to get out of bed, eat your breakfast, or chat with your friends. In fact, it's common for someone to feel tired or have lower energy when their mood is down.

Understanding Your Feelings

A **trigger** is something that sets off a negative emotional reaction in a person. Think of triggers as events or situations that make you feel uncomfortable, scared, or frustrated. Triggers can also make you feel lots of other emotions like embarrassment, worry, shame, and guilt.

When you're aware of your emotional triggers and have learned to identify them, you can more easily explain your feelings to someone else. You can also prepare ahead of time. Emotions are easier to manage when you are not surprised by them. Knowing your triggers also helps you get insight into other areas of life that you may be struggling with.

Know Your Triggers

Some people are triggered by being in loud situations, like a football game or concert. This is very common among autistic people. The sensory stimuli and distractions might make you feel uncomfortable or on edge. A **stimulus** is something in the environment, like a sound or sight, that triggers a response; it makes you feel or behave in a certain way. When a friend starts chatting with you during one of these events, you may feel overwhelmed and unable to carry on a conversation as you try to sort through all of the stimuli around you. If you already know that this type of environment is triggering for you, you may limit going to big, noisy events and make plans to spend time in quieter environments.

An upcoming social interaction that feels very difficult can also be triggering. For example, knowing that you'll have to sit at a dinner table with unfamiliar people or that you'll have to chat with extended family members at a family reunion might make you feel anxious. You may want to strategize ahead of time by thinking of questions or topics to bring up in conversation, or by finding a safe place to get some alone time to recharge when you need a break.

For some people, certain topics of conversation can be sensitive and triggering. For example, if you've been struggling with math despite having a tutor and putting extra time into studying, you may feel irritated when someone asks you how you are doing in your math class. Similarly, if you prefer more alone time, you may feel annoyed when your parents repeatedly suggest that you interact more with your siblings or with friends.

Generally, triggering topics are not intended to be hurtful. In fact, sometimes someone may be expressing interest in you by asking questions or bringing up subjects that seem important. But if you feel sensitive about the topic due to personal experience, these questions can make you feel uncomfortable.

Expressing Your Emotions

When you are triggered emotionally, you may have a strong reaction that takes you by surprise. It can be overwhelming and hard to communicate in the moment. Here are some tips for expressing strong emotions:

Take a deep breath. Pay attention to the bodily reactions you are experiencing because they give you clues about the emotion you are feeling. Is your heart beating fast? Do your muscles feel tense? Remember, we can't effectively express how we feel until we are aware of it.

Name your feeling. Identify if you are feeling sad, frustrated, angry, or uncomfortable.

Don't fight it. Sometimes we are so uncomfortable with a feeling that we start pushing it away in the moment. We try to ignore or deny the feeling altogether. This can make us feel even more uncomfortable. Accept the feeling.

Express it. Expressing an emotion can mean communicating it to someone else, or finding a healthy way to release it.

To communicate your emotions, try using phrases like, "I *feel* frustrated when . . ." or, "It makes me *feel* uncomfortable when . . ." By using language with the word *feel*, you're not blaming someone else or making an excuse. You are simply describing how you feel.

Try making your nonverbal communication *match* your words. For example, to communicate that you are uncomfortable, you might have a more serious facial expression, since it can be confusing if you smile when you express discomfort. Nonverbal cues can make it easier for the other person to understand your emotions.

Sometimes you may feel triggered even when there's no one around. For example, you might see something on social media that triggers you. You can express your emotions by journaling about how you feel, or by doing something fun, relaxing, or physical, like going for a walk or exercising. Research shows that physical activity can activate the good chemicals in the brain and makes you feel better.

EXERCISE: NAME THAT FEELING!

Let's practice some ways to communicate and express feelings. For each of the following emotions, choose all the sensations you experience when you feel that emotion. You can also write in your own experiences.

When you feel scared, what do you experience? (Circle everything that applies.)

- Sweating
- Shaking
- Fast heartbeat
- Tightness in the chest
- Tightness in the throat
- Dry mouth
- Upset stomach
- Other: _____

_____

When you feel angry, what do you experience?

- Hot face
- Clenching fists
- Tight jaw
- Headache
- Tightness in the chest
- Other: _____

_____

When you feel sad, what do you experience?

- Tiredness
- Headache
- Dizziness
- Muscle weakness

>

- Sore muscles
- Other: _____

_____

When you feel happy, what do you experience?

- Faster heartbeat
- Slower heartbeat
- Relaxed muscles
- Jitters or excitement
- High energy
- Other: _____

_____

Check in with a trusted adult to discuss your answers.

Responding to Other People's Emotions

We all show emotions in different ways. In fact, some people feel intense emotions but do not express them right away. They may want to process their feelings and discuss them later. In any case, it's important to detect other people's feelings when they try to communicate with you. When we notice and understand how other people feel, we can help them feel understood and supported.

Some people may use words to name their feelings. It's nice when someone does this because it takes some of the mystery out of detecting the feelings! More often, people use a combination of words and nonverbal strategies to convey their emotions. This can include their tone of voice, facial expressions, and body posture, as you learned in chapter 2.

How do we respond once we detect someone else's feelings? Our goal is to make sure the other person knows that we are listening, that we are trying to understand or that we "get it," and that we are there to help. Here are some important tips to keep in mind:

First, listen. Sometimes, when someone is feeling intense emotions, it helps to simply let them talk. You might feel tempted to jump in and fix the problem for them. You might also want to share something similar that you experienced, but the first step is to give the other person the space to talk and explain their feelings. Use your active listening skills and nonverbal cues, like looking at the person, leaning forward, and nodding your head (see chapter 2, page 27). Match the expression on your face with the other person's expression. For example, if they are looking serious or sad, you might have a concerned and serious look on your face, too.

Try to understand. It's okay to ask follow-up questions and to ask for clarification when someone is sharing their feelings. Doing so actually shows interest and investment in what they are saying.

Show that you care. Show that you really "get" how sad, scared, or irritated the other person is. You can say things like, "Wow, I can't believe that happened," "I'm so sorry you're dealing with that," or, "That must have been so hard!" At this point, it's okay to share something similar that happened to you. Keep this brief, though, so that you don't take away from what your friend is experiencing. You can say something like, "I think I know how you feel. Something similar happened to me when . . ." in one or two sentences, and then bring the focus back to your friend.

Offer help. Now it's time to ask what you can do to help. This doesn't mean that you have to fix the situation, but it's nice to offer your support. You can say something like, "Let me know if there is anything I can do," or, "I'm here if you need anything." It can also be helpful to think to yourself, "If this happened to me, what would I want my friend to do for me?"

Follow up. It's nice to let your friend know that you are thinking of them and care about them. You can do this the next time you see them in person, or you can send a message a few days after your conversation (or sooner, depending on how often you typically talk to them). Try saying something like, "I've been thinking of you. How are you doing since _____ happened?" or, "Just checking in! How are you feeling today?"

EXERCISE: HOW WOULD YOU RESPOND?

What would you say to your friend or someone you know in the following situations to show support and care?

- Your classmate just realized he forgot his homework at home, and he looks worried as he glances at the teacher.
- Your friend accidentally dropped her phone, and it broke. She's frowning and touching the broken phone screen.
- Your sister found out she didn't get invited to a get-together that she wanted to go to. She's looking at the floor and seems quieter than usual.
- One of your classmates failed an exam. He looks red in the face, his head is down, and he is not making eye contact with anyone.

Check in with a trusted adult to discuss your answers.

▶ REFLECTION QUESTIONS

- What do you feel in your body when you are angry? What about when you're anxious?
- What are some things you can do to prepare for the next time you're in a situation that makes you nervous, angry, or uncomfortable?
- What can you do to show you are listening and you care when someone shares negative feelings with you?

CHAPTER FIVE

CHECKING IN WITH YOURSELF

Checking in with yourself means taking the time to become aware of your own bodily responses and emotions before engaging with others. When you can identify what you're feeling, you can work on understanding and accepting your emotions. Being able to recognize and process feelings in real time takes practice, but this chapter will give you strategies to help you get started. In this chapter, you'll learn to accept your feelings even if they're uncomfortable to admit. You'll also learn how you can use your own thoughts, or "self-talk," to help manage your feelings.

- How aware are you of your body's physical signals and emotional responses?
- Which feelings feel most uncomfortable to you?
- Do you ever "check in" with yourself when you need a moment? Why or why not?

Noticing Changes in Your Body

When we recognize our emotions in our physical body, we are better able to process some of the negative feelings we have, like sadness, anger, or anxiety. For example, if someone says something hurtful to us, we might snap back at them defensively or say something equally hurtful. But if you are able to notice this feeling in your body right away, you can choose your words and reactions more carefully, which is more helpful to you and your relationship.

When you are triggered by someone's comment or by a specific situation, pause. Then locate the area of your body that is responding. Here are some check-in questions to help notice what signals your body is sending:

- Do you notice a tightness in your stomach?
- Do your hands get hot or sweaty when you are about to do something?
- Does your chest feel tight?
- Is your heart beating faster?
- Do you feel your arms or legs tighten?
- Is it difficult to relax your jaw?

If you answered yes to any of these questions, pause and reflect on your feelings. Did something happen to make you feel this way? If you're not sure why you're feeling these sensations, that's okay. Even if you're not sure what's causing them, it's important to accept these sensations for what they are. Then think about what you can do to help yourself feel more comfortable.

If you are in the middle of a conversation, you can say, "I'm sorry. Could we just sit quietly for a minute?" or excuse yourself from the situation for a moment to explore how you are feeling.

If you don't feel triggered by anything in the moment, you can still do a check-in with your body. Here's a technique called **body scan**, which can help you notice what is happening in your body. Body scan is one aspect of mindfulness, which helps us focus on the present moment and acknowledge and accept our feelings and thoughts.

1. Sit or lie down in a comfortable position. Close your eyes if you want.

2. Focus on your breath. Take five deep, slow breaths. How does your body feel as you breathe in? What about as you breathe out?

3. What sensations do you feel in your body? As you breathe in and out, how do your feet feel? What about your legs? Focus your attention on each part of your body through your torso, chest, and head, paying attention to how your body feels as you breathe in and out.

4. If your mind begins to wander, bring your attention back to your breathing.

5. Take a few more breaths, feeling your breath through your whole body.

6. Make a note of any sensations you feel in your body.

7. Make a note of any emotions you feel.

Noticing these sensations helps us become more aware of when our body reacts to something. In other words, we are tuned in when something triggers a change in our body, alerting us that we are experiencing a new emotion.

When you feel anxious, you may notice physical sensations in your stomach, chest, and palms.

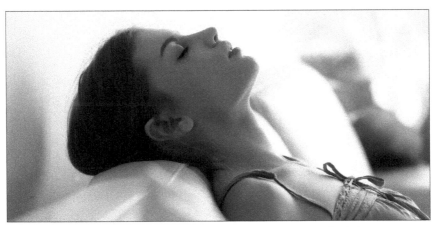

You can respond to unpleasant sensations in your body by practicing mindful breathing or doing a body scan.

Talking Back to Negative Self-Talk

When you experience emotions in your body, automatic thoughts or assumptions usually accompany your feelings. This is also called **self-talk**, which refers to any narrative or thoughts that stream through your head.

Negative self-talk happens when the voice inside your head sends you negative messages. One type of negative thought pattern is **catastrophic thinking**, or catastrophizing. When you catastrophize, you decide that the worst outcome will happen even though you don't know for sure. This makes you more likely to experience something in a negative way, and can also affect the way you interact with others.

Negative thoughts are usually not based on facts. We often jump to conclusions about why things happen or how something is going to turn out. We also make assumptions about how other people perceive us, even when we have no evidence for our theories. Sometimes we even act like we can read other people's minds when we really have no idea what others are actually thinking!

The good news is that we have control over our thoughts. We can counter negative thoughts with more positive thoughts. Positive self-talk addresses negative thinking in a rational way. At first, it can be hard to access positive thoughts in the moment, especially when we're feeling big emotions, so try practicing this when you are relaxed. Over time, you will get better at catching your negative self-talk as it happens.

Here's how to use positive self-talk:

Pause. Become aware of the physical sensations in your body.

Check in. How do these physical sensations connect with your emotions?

Notice negative self-talk. What assumptions are you making? Do you have any distorted thoughts? A **distorted thought** is a thought that isn't accurate, but that you have convinced yourself could be true. Distorted thoughts are usually negative.

Talk back to the negativity. Come up with more rational, positive thoughts that are based on evidence.

Feel better. Observe how positive self-talk can make you feel better about the situation.

Repeat. Practice makes perfect!

Come up with positive self-talk to respond to each of these negative thoughts. Include evidence for why the negative thought may not be accurate.

"He/She probably just came up to talk to me because he/she feels sorry for me."

Positive thought: _____

_____

_____

"I made a fool out of myself during my presentation, and now everyone in my class thinks I'm not smart."

Positive thought: _____

_____

_____

"Amy didn't text me back yet. She's probably annoyed with me."

Positive thought: _____

_____

_____

"Nobody liked the picture I posted an hour ago. I knew I shouldn't have posted it."

Positive thought: _____

_____

_____

Once you've become aware of your negative thoughts, write them down. For example, maybe you thought, "I dominated the conversation again. No wonder no one wants to talk to me." Recognize that this thought might be distorted. Then look at the evidence and facts to come up with a logical thought that is more reasonable. For example, it could be something like, "I may have talked a lot, so I will work on that. Jack texted me later on, so it's not true that *no one* wants to talk to me."

Because self-talk, or automatic thoughts, are *automatic*, it takes some practice to notice what's irrational about them and change them into positive thoughts. But it becomes easier the more you do it, so don't be discouraged!

Handling Stress

Stimming, also called **self-stimulatory behavior**, refers to the repetitive motor behaviors that some autistic people engage in. It may include hand flapping, rocking, spinning, bouncing, or saying the same things over and over. There are a lot of different theories as to why people "stim." Some propose that stimming helps people cope with stressful or overstimulating situations. Stimming can even help people concentrate or focus.

There is nothing wrong with stimming. In fact, it's helpful to have a way to calm your body and emotions. It's important to find safe places to stim so that you can have this outlet when you need it. But it might be hard to find the opportunity to stim during the day, especially if you are at school or work all day. When you get home, take some time to bounce, pace, or rock to self-soothe and decompress from the stress of the day. Stimming can help you recharge so that you can face the rest of the day.

Identifying Safe Spaces

If stimming helps you feel calm, it's important to identify safe places where you can do it. A safe place means a place where you can engage in stimming comfortably without detracting from being present in the moment.

If you are at school or work and feel the urge to stim, look at your schedule and identify times when you can be outside or have some time to yourself to self-soothe. For example, a quiet corner in the library or a private spot outside might be where you can feel calm. As long as you aren't hurting yourself physically, it's always okay to stim in the comfort of your own home.

A safe place can also be with your friends. If you are comfortable telling your friends about your desire to stim, you can stim when you are hanging out with them. Because not everyone stims, it can be confusing for someone if they see you rocking or jumping over and over. Talking to them about your stimming will make it seem less mysterious or unfamiliar.

For example, you can tell your friends that, just like some people feel better by going for a run, listening to music, or taking a shower to decompress or relax, you find that stimming helps you recharge and feel better. If you do stim with friends around, try engaging in subtler movements, like bouncing on the balls of your feet while standing in a group and talking, or squeezing a stress ball in your pocket.

Safe Stimming Methods

Because everyone's bodies and emotions are different, people respond to different stimming methods. Some find that pacing helps, whereas others find that bouncing repetitively works best. Make sure that your stimming doesn't cause physical injury, like banging your head against something hard. Otherwise, pacing, bouncing, rocking, or spinning can be a safe way to release tension when you have the space to do it.

If you don't have the space or privacy to engage in your preferred stimming method, try finding other ways to self-soothe until you have the opportunity to stim your way. For example, if you're sitting in class and would prefer to jump or bounce over and over again, see if it's possible to sit on a yoga ball or a "wiggle" seat cushion that allows you to move around slightly and get some of the input you need. You can also try rubbing a sensory toy like a prickly ball.

These alternatives may not give you the same satisfaction or soothe you in the same way as bigger body movements, but they may help you feel a little better by helping you focus on your surroundings until you can stim more later.

▶ REFLECTION QUESTIONS

- Are you aware of new sensations in your body that you weren't aware of before?
- What are your most common automatic thoughts? Are they connected to any negative feelings?
- How can you start using positive self-talk to feel better?
- Which stimming methods work best for you?
- What strategies have you used when you want to stim around others or when you don't have the space to stim? Are there new strategies you can implement after reading this chapter?

PART THREE

· · · · · · · · · · · · · · · · · · · ·

SOCIAL
SURVIVAL GUIDE

So far, you've learned strategies for taking care of yourself and managing different emotions. Now that you have a good grasp of communication basics and the kinds of friendships you might want, let's put what you have learned into practice. Part 3 will give you practical tips for handling social situations in different settings. You can use these tips to practice on your own or role-play with others so that you can get more comfortable with the strategies and figure out which approaches work best for you.

CHAPTER SIX

JOINING IN

Joining in with your peers by having conversations and hanging out together can be fun and rewarding. But it can be tricky and intimidating to break into a group. Some people compare this to watching a scene through a fishbowl, where you can see what's happening, but an invisible barrier seems to keep you from joining. Sometimes people feel more comfortable observing from afar, so they make excuses to justify why they don't join others. If the thought of joining in makes you anxious, avoiding it can give you immediate relief, but may lead to regrets or feelings of isolation later on. In this chapter, you'll get tips on how to show interest and have fun with others by learning how to enter an ongoing conversation, join a group of people engaged in an activity, or arrive at a get-together or party.

- What barriers keep you from joining in with your peers?
- What are some strategies you use to join a group of peers or enter a conversation with them?
- What are the benefits of joining in with your peers? What are some activities that are more fun to do with other people?

Getting Ready to Join

Before joining in with your peers, check in with yourself to make sure you want to join. It's okay if you don't feel like it! You also want to assess the situation and make sure the timing is right to join.

Do I Want to Join Right Now?

Joining is optional. Don't force yourself to join if you don't want to. The following tips are here for you if and when you *want* to join. *You* can decide when to engage with others.

Before you join in with others, consider your mood and energy level. Ask yourself:

- Do I feel ready to approach these friends?
- Am I feeling upset or angry about something?
- Do I need some time to recharge on my own?
- Does the thought of being around people right now energize me?
- Does the thought of being around people right now make me feel uncomfortable?

If you need alone time to recharge, that's okay. Once you've taken some time on your own and you feel ready, you'll probably be more motivated to engage with other people.

But sometimes, even when you're not up for interacting, you may *have* to interact. This is so hard! For example, let's say your parents invited the neighbors over for dinner. You may feel tired, and you just want to call it a day. But you know it would be impolite to disappear.

In this kind of situation, try to find the person you are most comfortable with and spend some time with them. It generally takes less effort to be with someone you are more familiar with. This might ease you into the situation and energize you so that you are more up for interacting with the other guests. Take breaks when you can (see chapter 5 on taking care of yourself).

Knowing When It's Okay to Join

How do you know if and when it's okay to join your peers? For example, how can you tell if it's okay to approach and join a group of kids at lunchtime or standing around talking after school?

Here are some signs to look for:

Open body language. Look at how people are standing or sitting with each other. Are they all huddled around each other, speaking quietly, or standing close together as they show each other something on a phone? Maybe they are talking about something private that is just between them. Or is there some physical distance between each of them as they all banter back and forth? If there's more physical space around each person and their postures seem more open, they are probably having a casual conversation about common topics. In this case, it might be okay for other people to jump in.

Facial cues. What about other nonverbal cues? Does everyone have a somber or serious look on their face? If so, they may be talking about something serious or personal, and this is not the time to join. Or are they laughing, showing that the conversation is more casual and lighthearted? When you glance over at the group, can you make eye contact with someone? This can be a sign that the group is welcoming other people to join. Making eye contact with someone is a good entry point, or opportunity for you to approach. But if the eye contact feels too short and the person looks away after it, you might want to look for other clues.

Not okay to join.

Okay to join.

Getting clues from the topic. If you're close enough, it's okay to briefly listen in to get an idea of what the group is talking about or what they're doing. Is it something you feel comfortable talking about or doing? Is the topic private (like about someone's family or a recent breakup), or is it more general (like about school or a movie)? If it's more private, you'll want to consider whether you are close enough friends to be a part of the conversation. If it's a more general topic, it's probably okay to join. If your peers are playing a game or eating lunch, make sure it's an activity that can accommodate more people, and that there is enough room for you to join in.

EXERCISE: TO JOIN OR NOT?

Here are some scenarios you might encounter with your peers. Would you feel okay joining?

- You see three of your peers standing close together. One of your peers hugs the other, and you can see that the one getting the hug is crying. Is it okay to join?
- A few of your peers are standing around after school, waiting to be picked up. You overhear them talking about what they're going to do on spring break. Is it okay to join?
- Two of your peers are playing cards at a lunch table. It looks intense! They are both really focused on the cards. Is it okay to join?

Check in with a trusted adult to discuss your answers.

How to Show Interest

Once you've found a good time to join in, there are strategies you can use to approach people in an appropriate way. One of the first things you can do is express interest.

When you show interest in others, they are more likely to reciprocate. Your peers may not know to chat with you or invite you to an activity if they don't know you are interested. We look for subtle signs in other people to gauge whether they're interested and motivated to hang out.

You can show people you're interested in joining them by doing the following:

Pay compliments. When it comes to joining in, people want to know if you're friendly and interested. Paying a compliment is a good way to break in and put someone at ease. Make it brief, like, "Nice shot," to someone playing basketball, or, "Cool shirt." You don't have to lie if you don't actually like the shirt. Look for positive things in others that you can say something nice and sincere about.

Look for shared interests. Making conversation is always a bit easier when you have a shared interest you can talk about. Before joining, think about what you have in common with your peers. (Are you on a sports team together? Are you in the same class? Do you share an interest or hobby?) If you're meeting someone new, use body language and nonverbal behaviors (facing the person, making eye contact, nodding your head, and smiling) to show interest. Follow up with relevant questions or comments on what the other person said.

Learn and remember someone's name. When you meet someone for the first time, like when a mutual friend introduces you to someone new, you'll learn each other's names right away. If you repeat the name by saying, "Nice to meet you, John," this can help you remember the name. It also shows that you are paying attention and that the person is important to you. Other times, you might join in with a group and engage in a conversation before being introduced. For example, you see one of your friends talking with two other people. When the time is right, you approach them and join in. When there's a pause in the conversation, you can say, "I'm Jack, by the way," which will prompt the others to introduce themselves as well.

Approaching Someone You Know

Let's say you spot someone you know at the grocery store and you want to acknowledge them.

▷ **Desired Outcome:** You'd like to greet them, have a brief conversation, and then end the conversation at the right time.

Give nonverbal cues. Make eye contact and smile. Wave if the person is more than several feet away. (You don't want to shout, "Hey!" across the grocery store if the person is all the way at the end of an aisle).

Approach. Once you've acknowledged the person using nonverbal cues, make your way over to them. Put a pause on your shopping (it might feel awkward to acknowledge the person and then search for your cereal), but do bring your basket or cart with you. Once you approach, remember your space bubble and leave at least an arm's-length of space between you (unless the store is really crowded).

Say a greeting. Give a greeting like, "What's up?" or, "Good to see you!" Make sure to smile to convey your excitement (and maybe surprise), and use a tone of voice that conveys some enthusiasm for running into the other person unexpectedly.

Have a brief conversation. This is a casual situation in public, so it's probably not the time for a long, intimate conversation. When you run into someone in public unexpectedly, keep the conversation brief, from less than a minute to a couple of minutes at the most. Start by making a comment about the grocery store, like, "This place is the best, right? I come here for the smoothie bar." Or ask a question about their experience: "How's your weekend been so far?" or, "Is this your neighborhood store?" If you're shopping during a virus or flu outbreak, wave and say a quick hello without stopping.

End the conversation. Every once in a while, old friends run into each other at the grocery store and end up chatting for a long time. But more often, people run into an acquaintance and have a brief exchange and then continue shopping. If you see the other person beginning to look around the store, review their shopping list, or grab more items as you're talking, it probably means they are itching to keep moving. Even if they aren't giving you these cues, be mindful that people tend to have limited time at the store. End the conversation by saying something like, "It was great running into you!" or, "Enjoy the rest of your shopping!" to signal that you're ready to end the conversation. If you run into them a few minutes later, simply wave and smile this time.

Approaching a Group

Imagine that you see people you know in the hallway at school. They haven't seen you yet, but you want to approach them to say hi.

▷ **Desired Outcome:** Your goal is to approach your peers while giving them a heads-up that you're approaching. You'd like to greet them and have a brief exchange or just acknowledge each other with a wave.

Catch someone's eye. If someone in the group is facing your general direction, make eye contact and smile and/or nod your head in acknowledgment. If they aren't facing your direction, keep walking until you're in their line of vision. Be sure they can see you approaching to avoid surprising anyone.

Approach and greet. Walk toward the group. If they are in the middle of a conversation, make eye contact and wave and smile as you walk by. You can say, "Hey," "What's up?", or "How are you?" as you pass. These phrases can be used as a greeting, and they don't necessarily signal the start of a conversation. These short greetings can also let you know if they're open to chatting more or including you in the conversation.

Brief exchange. If there happens to be a pause in the group's conversation, you may get a few responses to your greeting. If someone puts their hand out for a handshake or asks you a specific question, this is probably a signal for you to slow down and have a brief exchange. In this situation, there will be a natural ending to the conversation when the bell rings or your peers start to disperse to their next class or activity.

No exchange. You may give a brief greeting and get no response or just a quick glance in your direction. If this is the case, continue to smile and keep walking by. This might feel like a rejection, especially if you *assume* everyone saw you and chose not to respond. But consider other possible explanations: They may have been engrossed in a conversation or about to rush off to class. Perhaps the hallway was too crowded, and they didn't really notice your greeting. If the timing wasn't right, keep moving and try again next time.

Having Fun

Interacting with others through conversations or a shared activity can be fun and rewarding. Entering a conversation is one of the first steps to getting to know someone. Conversing and engaging in shared activities help you assess whether you'd like to get to know someone more and ultimately whether you'd like to be their friend. (This applies to dating too!)

Entering a Conversation

Entering a conversation or joining an activity with people you don't know well can be intimidating and make you feel vulnerable. You might think, "What if they don't want to talk to me? What if I don't know what to say?" Let's explore some strategies to help you feel more comfortable and confident when joining conversations.

Imagine a scenario where several people are talking excitedly about a movie you just watched.

▶ **Desired Outcome:** You'd like to approach the group and contribute an interesting tidbit or have fun talking about the movie. This means merging into the group by approaching them, discreetly listening to their conversation, and identifying the right time to ask a relevant question or make a comment.

> **Know your audience.** Identify the people in the group. Do you know any of them already? Can you think of something you have in common? In this case, you are already familiar with the movie they're talking about!

> **Observe.** Spend a few minutes observing and listening. Sort through your backpack or check something in your folder so that you appear "busy," giving yourself a little time while you evaluate. What are they saying about the movie?

> **Filter negative thoughts.** Take a moment to check your assumptions. For example, are you assuming they won't want you to join or that you aren't going to have anything meaningful to add?

Consider whether you actually have any evidence for this thinking, or if your negative thoughts are keeping you from trying. Take a deep breath and expect a good outcome.

Break through. Wait for a brief pause and then try one of these ways to break in:

- Nod and acknowledge your peers with a smile and eye contact or with a short phrase like, "What's up?"
- Make a comment about the topic of conversation like, "I loved that part of the movie, too!"
- Ask a relevant question.

Keep contributing. If you're not sure what to say next, take your time by using some of your nonverbal strategies like nodding and making eye contact. Wait until there is another brief pause and you feel like you can make another comment or ask a question.

This would be a great time to practice the conversation skills you learned in chapter 2.

Joining an Activity

Two people are playing a game that you want to join. Imagine a video game at someone's house, shooting hoops on a basketball court, or a card or chess game at school.

▶ **Desired Outcome:** You'd like to signal interest to the other two people and be invited, or you want to ask to join them and be accepted.

Observe. Just like entering a conversation, give yourself a moment to get a sense of the activity and the interaction before trying to join. You can do something to appear "busy" like checking your phone while you listen to the other two people. Is this a game you're familiar with? Can more than two people play?

Filter negative thoughts. Look out for any negative thoughts you have. Sometimes you can sabotage yourself before taking the leap because negative thoughts tell you things like, "They probably don't need a third person there," or, "Looks like they're having enough fun without me; if they wanted me there, they would have asked." In reality, you don't know if any of those assumptions are true. Even if they are having fun already, they might want to mix it up by having another person join! You won't know until you ask.

Time it right. You don't want to jump in and distract them mid-shot or when someone is about to block a winning move. Once you have a sense of the game, wait until there is a natural break (after someone's turn is over or they take a quick break to regroup).

Approach. Go up to the two people, but stop a few feet from them. If you go right up to them and sit down at their game or jump right onto the court, you are assuming it's okay to play. Remember that you haven't been invited or asked to join yet.

Ask a question or make a comment. Once you're close enough and you've made eye contact with one of your peers, make a comment about the game. Remember, one way to break in is to compliment one of the players by saying something like, "Nice move." This can signal interest, and you may be asked if you want to play. If not, you can ask more directly. Depending on how the game works (does it accommodate three players or do you have to wait a turn?), you can ask something like, "You guys up for a third player?" or, "Can I jump in next?"

Respond positively. Whether you are asked to join, told you can join in a few minutes, or told that they don't need a third, accept their response by smiling and responding with something like, "Cool!" or, "No worries, maybe next time."

No matter what happens, you've shown interest by approaching them, which is great. They might be more likely to invite you again if you show that you can go with the flow.

Entering a Party

A party full of people can be really intimidating to walk into, but potentially really fun once you're in it! Here are some tips.

▶ **Desired Outcome:** You want to enter a busy party and find someone you're comfortable talking to.

Check your assumptions. Many people have negative thoughts about joining a party, especially if arriving by themselves. It's common to have thoughts about how awkward it might feel to walk in on your own, doubts about whether you really want to join, or fears about what might happen if you can't find someone you know right away. Remember that most people are focused on their own experience and won't be watching you as you walk in. Having a game plan will help.

Manage your anxiety. If you feel a bit anxious about joining a party, take a minute to calm your body before going in. Take some deep breaths and try to come up with some positive thoughts about the experience. For example, remind yourself that you usually have a good time once you join, or that you can always take breaks if you need to.

Observe discreetly. Once you enter, take a moment to observe the party. Again, you can pretend to look at your phone or check out the invitation while you observe. Try to find a familiar person and make it your goal to approach them first. If you can't find someone you know, try to find something to do. For example, locate a sign-in table or the name tags, and make those your first stop. If you know that a friend is already at the party, text them to let them know you're there. Agree to meet at a specific spot.

Walk into the party. Once you have a game plan, use open and confident body language: head up, shoulders back, and arms at your side. Make sure your facial expression is welcoming by smiling. Even if you don't really have a reason to smile yet, that's okay. You don't want to look like it's a chore to enter a party, even if you've felt that way in the past!

Approach. When you see a familiar person, greet them with enthusiasm. Say, "Hi! How's it going?" or, "How's the party so far?" Remember, it's okay to take breaks if you need to throughout the party.

Making Plans

Let's say you want to go see a movie with friends.

▶ **Desired Outcome:** Your goal is to schedule a movie outing with your friends and for everyone to show up and have fun.

Decide whom to ask. You might have a group of friends that you regularly hang out with, so choosing whom to invite may be easy. If you're looking to make new friends, planning a get-together outside school can be a great bonding experience that lets you get to know them better. If you're inviting a few friends to the movies, make sure to choose friends who like movies. (Have you heard them talk about movies before? Have you seen movies with them before?) Choose people who may like the same type of movie you do.

Pick a movie. Have a movie in mind that you want to see with your friends, but also have back-up options in case some of them have already seen it or they're not interested in seeing it. It can be hard to be flexible, especially when you really want to see a certain movie! Remember that the point of scheduling an outing with friends is to spend time with them and have fun doing something that is enjoyable for everyone. You can always see your preferred movie another time.

Schedule the outing. When you ask your friends about seeing a movie, have a general time frame in mind. For example, ask if they would be up for seeing a movie "next weekend." If you are too specific ("Saturday at 4 p.m."), it's possible that your friends could say no if they have other plans that afternoon. They may be interested in going but can't because of the time. If you leave the date and time a little open-ended, you have the opportunity to discuss timing that works for everyone, making the outing more likely to happen!

Decide on the date and time. Make sure everyone is on the same page about which movie, where you are seeing it, and on what day and time. Repeat the logistics back to everyone before ending the conversation or text chain. ("So, *X-Men* on Sunday at 1 p.m. Great!") If you are purchasing tickets electronically, make a plan for one person to buy them and everyone else to pay them back, or coordinate your seats if you're all purchasing them separately.

Follow up. A few hours before the movie, text your friends. This is a subtle way to remind everyone about the plans and to make sure nothing has changed with the original plan. You can also update plans, like suggesting an exact meeting spot. Text something brief and upbeat, like, "Looking forward to seeing you guys at the mall for *X-Men*! Meet outside the theater at 12:50?"

Asking Someone to Hang Out

You'd like to invite someone to hang out at a new ice cream shop that just opened.

▶ **Desired Outcome:** You want to ask someone to get ice cream sometime and make plans with them.

Choose someone to ask. It can be hard to tell who would be open to hanging out with you. Generally, make sure the person is within your age group and has some common interests, and that you know them from school, from the neighborhood, through family or a mutual friend, or from another shared activity. You can never be sure who is interested in being friends, but usually you can ask someone to hang out if you have already had at least a few conversations with them and they seem interested in talking to you, having done things like asking more questions and sharing information.

Ask in private. If you're trying to make plans with one friend, don't talk about plans when you're in a group conversation with other people. You don't want anyone to feel left out. Ask your friend when it's just the two of you talking. If you're asking via text, make sure you're making plans in a one-on-one conversation rather than a group chat.

Feel it out. Before getting into the details of planning, try to get a sense of whether the other person is open to hanging out. For example, maybe mention the new ice cream shop and ask if the person has been there yet. Or mention that you may grab ice cream over the weekend since it's supposed to be hot out. If the other person asks more about going to get ice cream, that could be a sign of interest. But if the other person changes the subject, maybe they're not interested.

Present a general idea. Similar to making plans to go to the movies with your friends, leave the details open so the other person isn't stuck with just one option. For example, if you ask, "Want to get ice cream at 1 p.m. Sunday?" and they say, "No," you can't be sure whether they are saying no in general, or no because they're not available at that time. Keep it open-ended by saying something like, "We should try that place sometime," or, "Want to grab ice cream at the new shop sometime this weekend?" Using a word like *sometime* leaves the timing open so that your friend has more of an opportunity to work out a plan.

Agree on specifics. If you're hanging out for the first time, plan on meeting at the ice cream shop. Share contact information in case anything changes with the plans. Just like you would when planning for a movie with a group of friends, repeat the plan back before ending the conversation to make sure you're both on the same page. (Tip: Tell a trusted friend or family member what the plans are, too. It's always good for someone else to know where you are and whom you're with, especially if you're still getting to know someone new.)

Follow up. The evening before or the morning of, send a brief, upbeat text like, "Looking forward to seeing you at the ice cream shop! I'll meet you right outside at 3."

Keep it simple. If this is the first time you're hanging out, don't add more activities. Getting ice cream or coffee is a great way to have an initial meetup and get to know each other without added pressure. If you're having a great time at the ice cream shop, you can always choose to hang out for longer another time. It's easier to make more plans than it is to cancel in the middle of a long day!

▶ REFLECTION QUESTIONS

- What are some negative thoughts you've had before joining in? How do they get in the way of entering conversations or activities?
- What are some upcoming situations where you can practice joining in? (Research suggests that the more we do things, the more comfortable we feel; practicing ahead of time helps with this!)
- In which situations do you feel most comfortable joining in? How do you feel when you're chatting with just a few friends, joining a video game, or arriving at a big activity like a party?

CHAPTER SEVEN

UNEXPECTED SITUATIONS

When your plans don't pan out the way you expect, things can get pretty awkward or upsetting. When you're thrown off your routine or when a social interaction doesn't go the way you planned, you might find it hard to accept the situation and stay flexible. No matter how much you prepare, unexpected and uncomfortable situations will happen, but having strategies will help you go with the flow. In this chapter, you'll get step-by-step tips to help you get through these difficult moments.

- Can you think of unexpected situations in the past that were hard to deal with?
- How does it feel when you're thrown off your routine?
- Have you ever been in the middle of a social interaction like a conversation and had something unanticipated come up, like a disagreement?

Changes to Routine

We all have routines or systems to help us through the day. For example, you may have a morning routine in which you do things in a certain order, like take a shower, brush your teeth, and then eat breakfast. If something disrupts your routine (maybe your sister is hogging the bathroom), it can throw you off and make you feel stressed out.

Some of us are more attached to our routines than others. Some autistic people, for example, tend to like predictability. Small, unexpected changes can make them feel upset or anxious. Here are some strategies to help you go with the flow when things don't go as you expected.

Going with the Flow

You probably juggle lots of transitions throughout a regular school day. You might go from one class to another, stop at your locker, and manage exams and other activities that pop up throughout the week. Over time, you learn to manage your schedule.

But what happens when you show up at school and there is a substitute teacher? Or maybe there is an assembly during history, which is your favorite class. How do you deal with these sudden changes?

Let's say you have a substitute teacher or have to face other changes at school.

▷ **Desired Outcome:** React calmly when you find out about the change. Roll with the changes throughout the day.

Help your body calm down. When you first find out about an unexpected change, you might feel your heart start pounding or heat run through your body. Chances are this unexpected turn of events has caused some anxiety. Use the strategies you learned in chapter 5 to take some deep breaths. If possible, take a quick break by walking outside.

Identify what's bothering you. Take a moment to assess what is really making you feel distressed. Is it that your favorite teacher lets you take extra time on an assignment and the substitute won't know about this arrangement? Does missing history class mean that you don't get to watch the rest of the documentary you were watching the day before? Figure out what is really going to be different about your day. Most likely, your day won't necessarily be worse, just a bit different. Notice whether you are catastrophizing about how bad things will be because of the change.

Visualize your day going smoothly. Even though your day won't be what you expected, it can still go smoothly. Picture yourself going from class to class feeling calm. It's like writing a story in your head with a happy and successful ending. How does the day turn out if it goes well? Do you get the support you need from your substitute teacher? Do you figure out an alternative plan for your history class? How does it feel to visualize a positive outcome?

Problem-solve. Once you pinpoint what's causing your distress and what a successful day would look like, brainstorm what you can do about it. Maybe you could let the substitute teacher know about accommodations you typically get, or ask your history teacher when you'll get to watch the rest of the documentary. Most of the time, you can still get to do what you want, though it may take some problem-solving to make it happen.

Express your needs. In this case, if you've identified how to solve the problem, you may need to communicate your needs to a teacher. You might feel really eager to solve the problem, but make sure to wait until the time is appropriate and you're not interrupting anything, such as before class, when there is a break, or when you have the opportunity to ask a question privately.

Being Open to Options

You always eat a certain food item at lunch, but it's not available, and you feel bothered. This could happen at school or when you're out to lunch with friends. When this takes you by surprise, especially if you've been looking forward to your favorite food, it can really throw you off.

▷ **Desired Outcome:** Choose the next best option and enjoy your lunch.

Respond calmly. You might be caught off guard and disappointed, but you want to show that you can move on, especially in public. If you say something lighthearted like, "Oh, bummer," you acknowledge that you're disappointed but that it's no biggie. Accept that you'll have to make a new choice.

Choose something new. It might be hard to pick something else if you hadn't planned on it. Remember, this is not your only meal of the day! You can probably get a snack later, and you'll have dinner. So, even if it's not your favorite, getting the next best option is okay. Maybe you'll discover a new favorite.

Make the best of it. You might wonder what happened; did they run out of your favorite choice? Maybe you wish you had known ahead of time so that you could have prepped for a new choice. But now that doesn't really matter. Once you've chosen something else, focus on your friends or your relaxing break time and enjoy your lunch.

Staying open and flexible lets you have more fun while navigating different situations, especially when you're building friendships.

Handling Disappointment

Let's say you are usually in charge of feeding your dog. It's part of your daily routine to feed the dog when you get home from practice in the evening. You always look forward to it, so you're totally thrown off when you get home and find out your brother has already done it.

▷ **Desired Outcome:** Acknowledge your brother for helping with the chore even though you prefer to do it yourself.

> **Express your feelings.** In this case, since you're dealing with someone you know very well and you're at home, it's okay to be more open about your disappointment. Tell your brother that you had expected to feed the dog as you usually do as part of your routine. Let him know that even though he may have been trying to help, this throws you off since it didn't match your expectations. For example, you can tell him, "I'm bummed because I was expecting to feed him when I got home, like I always do."

> **Check your assumptions.** If you assume your brother had bad intentions, you might feel even more upset. What are some legitimate reasons your brother might have fed the dog? Maybe your dog seemed hungry, so he fed him. Or maybe he knows you're tired when you come home, so he wanted to help you with your chore. If you assume that he had good intentions, it might help you feel a little better and make it easier to deal with the change in your routine. Even though your evening turned out a little differently than you'd expected, it's not necessarily worse. Hopefully, you can still get some one-on-one time with your dog.

> **Acknowledge your brother's help.** Once you've expressed how you feel in a calm way, acknowledge that you understand that your brother was trying to help. You can tell him, "Thank you for trying to help," or, "I appreciate that you fed the dog when he was hungry."

When you gently acknowledge your disappointment and clearly express what you prefer, your brother will be more willing to consider your preferences in the future. Practicing how to handle difficult feelings in this way can help you navigate tricky moments with your friends and family.

Navigating Differences

Sometimes things don't go quite how we expect with our friends. You may assume you're on the same page and have the same opinions about something, and then be caught by surprise when your friend sees something in a different way. Or maybe you and your friend had plans to do something together, and your friend had a different idea or expectation of how the afternoon would go. How do you address these differences while still maintaining a positive social interaction?

Handling Disagreements

Imagine a situation in which you and your friend are discussing a movie or book. Your friend says they hate something that you love. The disagreement can make a social interaction feel uncomfortable. For example, you're a huge *Star Wars* fan and love talking to people about *Star Wars*. Your friend has seen the movies, so you assume they liked *Star Wars*, too. During a conversation, they make a comment about hating the most recent movie that came out, which you loved! You're caught off guard.

▷ **Desired Outcome:** Respond with humor or curiosity, not anger or frustration; reach a compromise.

> **Ask a question.** You might be surprised that your friend disagrees with you, and this can make you feel defensive or even confused. By asking for clarification, you show that you're open to their thoughts and opinions. You can ask, "What don't you like about it?"

> **Use active listening.** Make eye contact if you can. Nod your head every now and then while your friend explains their perspective. You may not agree, but their view is still important. By

giving them time and attention, you're showing that you care about them, whether or not they agree with you.

Show curiosity. Ask follow-up questions like, "Do you like the older *Star Wars* movies better?" You can smile and tell your friend, "Okay, may the Force be with you!" or something funny to defuse any tension.

Compromise. You can both have valid viewpoints on this, so try to acknowledge that you can both be a little right. Acknowledge that maybe certain movies in the series are better than others, so if the last one wasn't his favorite, you can understand that. Reaching a compromise means you're meeting somewhere in the middle.

You don't have to change your opinions just to make someone else feel better. And this works the other way around. Other people don't have to agree with you, even if you believe that they're mistaken.

Changing Plans

You thought you and your friend had plans to go to the movies on Saturday, but she invited along another friend, and they decided on bowling instead.

▶ **Desired Outcome:** Go with the flow by accepting the change in plans and still have fun.

Ask for clarification. It's okay to express some confusion and ask what happened to the initial plan. For example, say to your friend, "Oh, I thought we had talked about going to the movies. Did something change?" Get the information you need about the new plan.

Self-check. Once you know what the new plan is, ask yourself if you're comfortable with it. The fact that it's not what you planned might be the most distressing part of it. You might enjoy bowling, but if it's not what you expected, it might seem stressful.

It's your choice. If you think you could enjoy bowling, consider going with the new plan. If you're not sure you will enjoy bowling but you still want to hang out with your friends, just go for it. Reasons for not going with the new plan would include concerns about your safety or a scheduling conflict (for example, the timing of the new plan interfering with a family obligation).

Go with it. Assuming the new plan is safe and works out okay logistically, tell your friends you're open to giving it a try. Express some enthusiasm by saying something like, "Sure, I'm up for that!" to show that you're not bitter about the change.

You never have to go with a friend's plan if you aren't comfortable with it. And it's okay to speak up for what you want (see chapter 8). But if the new plan is safe and you want to hang out with your friends, go for it!

AGREE TO DISAGREE

Disagreements can be uncomfortable because most of us like to be right! Compromising with someone means that you meet somewhere in the middle. You might not get exactly what you want or convince the other person that you are totally right, but you *compromise* by accepting their perspective, too.

For example, you want to eat dinner at 6 p.m. every night because that gives you more time to wind down and get your work done after dinner. Your sister prefers 7 p.m. because she prefers to get things done *before* dinner. A compromise would be to eat dinner at 6:30. Although this is a bit different from what you wanted, you accept that your sister also has valid reasons for wanting dinner later, and you meet somewhere in the middle. Your sister's priorities are important, too. When you value your relationship or friendship with someone, you need to be willing to accept that you can disagree on what's *right*, but find a way to compromise.

Rule Breakers

Rules help us know what type of behavior is appropriate and safe, so it's nice to have them as guidelines. For example, waiting until you see a walk signal before crossing the street is an important rule to follow because it keeps you safe. Other rules help keep order, like raising your hand before speaking in class so that everyone isn't shouting at once.

Rules are also helpful because they make things more predictable. If there is a rule that you take shoes off before going in your house, you know the first thing you'll do when you open the front door. It's nice to know what to expect.

Knowing and following the rules might be important to you. But sometimes, people *don't* follow the rules. For example, maybe someone doesn't sit in their assigned seat when they get to class or they don't throw their lunch out when they're done eating. It can be hard when people don't act the way they're supposed to. It might even be so annoying that you feel like you have to correct others so that they know and follow the rules. But it doesn't have to be your job to remind others about following the rules.

When Someone Litters

Let's say you saw a student litter in the classroom. There is a clear rule that you don't litter in class (or anywhere), so this is distressing to you.

▶ **Desired Outcome:** Politely point out the litter to the other student, or just let the issue go and throw the litter out yourself.

Give the benefit of the doubt. Sometimes people make mistakes, so start by assuming the student littered by accident. Maybe that isn't the case, but taking this perspective will make you sound a bit gentler and politer when you point out the issue.

Politely point it out. For example, you can say, "Oops, did you drop that?" or, "Oh, I think you might have missed something."

This gives the other person an opportunity to fix their mistake without feeling criticized or reprimanded. (A reprimand would sound something like, "You littered, and that's not allowed.")

Throw it out yourself. The student may throw away their trash after you politely point it out. But if they don't, it's no big deal. When you're throwing out your own trash, you can throw theirs out, too. By grabbing it on your way to the trash can, you come across as being helpful while still following the rules.

There may be other times you notice your peers doing something that is against the rules. Someone may take up a whole bench on the bus when they're supposed to share, sneak candy in the middle of class, or whisper in class when they're not supposed to be talking. If the rules are important to you, you may feel unsettled when you see other people not following them. In general, it's best to let these things go, since it's not your job to remind others of the rules.

When Someone Cuts in Line

Let's say you're in line to buy lunch and someone cuts in front of you.

▶ **Desired Outcome:** Politely point it out and/or stay in line patiently.

Give the benefit of the doubt. Just as in the litter example, assume the person made a mistake. Maybe they didn't see you or didn't realize where the line ended. Remember, assuming it was an honest mistake will help you avoid overreacting.

Politely point it out. You may want to consider whether it's worth saying anything. In this case, will one extra person in line change your day that much? It might be hard to wait an extra minute, but maybe the line moves quickly and it won't be a big deal. On the other hand, if you have been waiting a long time or you are in a big rush, it may be worth saying something like, "Sorry, the end of the line is actually back there." (A reprimand or accusation would sound more like, "Hey! You're cutting!" This would most likely lead to a conflict.)

Stay in line patiently. As uncomfortable as it can be when someone cuts, wait it out. Your turn may take a little more waiting than you had expected, but it will come!

Other Distractions

You're standing in line waiting to go inside after PE, and some kids are fooling around in line. You might be really bothered by the other kids who aren't following the rules. It might be annoying or distracting, especially when you're trying your best to follow the rules.

▶ **Desired Outcome:** Let it go and keep following the rules.

Assess the situation. Is it worth calling out? In the previous example, the person cutting you in line made you wait longer. It's okay to stand up for yourself and point it out. In this case, kids are misbehaving, but *you* can still go along doing your own thing. Their behavior doesn't really get in your way.

Keep doing your own thing. As annoyed as you might be, try to just do your own thing. If the behavior is really problematic, it's the teacher's job to let the other students know.

When you feel bothered by other people's behaviors, focusing on yourself is usually a good strategy, especially if they're not harming you or other people.

WHY PEOPLE DON'T LIKE TATTLETALES

When other people break the rules, it can be stressful. They're not doing what they're supposed to be doing, and you feel the urge to point it out! But is it always the best move to tell on someone?

For example, you notice that two students in class are whispering and showing each other pictures on a phone while everyone is supposed to be doing an assignment. You know phones are not allowed during class time. Is it your job to tell the teacher? Let's think this through.

If you tell the teacher, what are the consequences? Most likely, the other students will get in trouble. What does that mean for you? How will the other students view you? They may blame you for getting them in trouble, since you're the one who pointed out their misbehavior.

In most cases, it's best to just focus on your own work and wait until the teacher notices (or not). It would be a bummer if you were seen as a tattletale and other kids resented you for it. On the other hand, if you see something that isn't safe (like someone having a weapon at school or a student bullying another student), that's worth telling. Safety is a priority. Otherwise, best to try to let it go!

Feeling Left Out

When your friends leave you out, it can hurt. On top of the surprise and the unexpected change of plans, you're sad that they wouldn't consider you before making plans. How do you handle these situations?

When Friends Hang Out without You

You're used to eating lunch with the same group of people every day, and one day they all leave campus for lunch without telling you. You feel hurt and start to wonder what you could have done to make them exclude you.

▶ **Desired Outcome:** Express how you feel and join them next time.

Clarify what happened. Misunderstandings happen, and it could be that leaving you out was unintentional. (Remember to give the benefit of the doubt!) Ask your friends what happened. You can do this over text or when you see them after lunch. Say something like, "Hey, what happened at lunch? I missed you guys." By asking a question rather than accusing with a statement like, "You ditched me at lunch," you're creating an opening for conversation.

Express how you feel. Use "I" statements to express how you felt by saying something like, "I was bummed that I didn't know," or, "I would've loved to go, too." This is not an accusation or attack. When you're not sure what to say, avoid saying sentences that start with *you*, like, "You were so rude."

Plan for next time. Suggest that next time, someone should send a group text before lunch, or decide on a time or place so that there are no surprises. Tell your friend directly, "Text me if you guys are going again tomorrow."

When You Feel Left Out of a Conversation

Your friends are talking about a topic you don't know about, so you feel left out. Sometimes we wish we could prepare ahead of time for conversations so that topics don't catch us off guard. But usually, we don't know what to expect. How can you manage the fear of missing out when this happens?

▶ **Desired Outcome:** Figure out a way to join the conversation or gracefully make an exit.

Actively listen. Others may simply not know that you're not familiar with the topic. They can't read your mind! It's okay to fake it at first by paying attention and following the conversation using nonverbal strategies (nodding your head) and verbal cues ("mm-hmm").

Ask a question. Sometimes you might worry that asking a question will show that you don't know what's going on. But you can also ask questions to show interest. Doing so is a good way to get into the conversation when you don't know a lot about the topic, or even when you have no idea what's going on. Ask something about the person's experience rather than a specific detail about the topic. For example, if everyone is talking about a new movie and you don't know anything about it, you can ask, "Did you see it at the new theater?" or, "When did you see it?" You might even ask them if it's similar to a movie you're more familiar with.

Engage in conversation. If you're comfortable in the conversation, keep listening actively, asking relevant questions and comments.

Make an exit. If it's too hard to engage in the conversation and you want to head out, that's okay. Let your friends know that you have to go by telling them something like, "I've got to run—see you guys later." You don't have to tell them that you don't like the topic. Make sure to make eye contact; as you walk away, turn, wave, and smile.

No matter how much you prepare for things, unexpected changes will happen, and people will do things that you don't anticipate. This can be really hard if you're the kind of person that likes things to be predicable. But if you know this about yourself, you already have an understanding of what's bothering you when something unexpected does happen. Knowing your triggers and your feelings is the first step in being able to problem-solve and deal with the change. Remember, change is not always bad; it's just different!

- How can you go with the flow if your routine is thrown off at school? How will you deal with surprises as they come up?
- How can you decide whether it's worth pointing out when someone breaks a rule?
- Can you think of some examples in your life where it would be helpful to compromise (rather than trying to prove that you're right)?

CHAPTER EIGHT

HANDLING CONFRONTATIONS

A confrontation happens when there is a misunder-standing or argument between two people. Many people are uncomfortable with confrontations because they can feel unpleasant. But sometimes confrontations are unavoidable because you have to address a problem—for example, if someone is upset with you and wants to talk about it, or if someone continues to demand something from you after you've said no. In these situations, you want to be able to engage with the other person in a pro-ductive way or even stand up for yourself if needed. In this chapter, we will review tips for handling confronta-tions with others and what to do if things escalate.

- Can you think of a time when you've had a confrontation with someone else? How did it go?
- Do you ever avoid confrontations with others?
- How do you respond when someone pressures you to do something you're not comfortable with?

Dealing with Criticism

No one likes being criticized. It's really difficult when someone points out something you did wrong or makes a negative comment about you. Sometimes we need feedback (like when a coach gives you pointers on how to improve your swing), but other times it can feel like an insult (like when someone comments on your clothing style). We can't always control what people say to us, but we can control how we deal with it. Here are some tips for dealing with criticism.

Brushing Off Opinions

Say you're at the dinner table and you tell the same joke a few times, making sure everyone understands why it's funny. Your brother tells you that your jokes are not funny.

▷ **Desired Outcome:** Express how you feel about his comment and move on.

Watch your reactions. If someone says your jokes aren't funny, your knee-jerk or automatic reaction might be to be defensive and say something like, "Your jokes are even more boring!" But this would lead to more conflict between you and your brother, leaving you both feeling bad.

Consider the context. You and your brother might give each other a hard time on a regular basis. Is this another random comment that he's making to get under your skin? If so, it might be worth it to say something like, "Okay, whatever," and move on. (See chapter 9 for more tips on dealing with teasing.) But if you consider yourself a good joke-teller and his criticism is particularly hurtful, it's probably worth expressing how his comment impacts you.

Express how you feel. Try telling your brother that you feel hurt when he criticizes you. If you're too upset in the heat of the moment, wait until you feel a bit calmer. Let him know that you were just trying to make everyone laugh and that his criticism stings.

When people are criticized, they tend to want to attack back. Most of the time, it's best to respond without overreacting.

Taking Feedback

You worked really hard on an English paper, but your teacher gave you a lot of negative feedback on your writing. You meet with her after class to discuss all of the comments.

▶ **Desired Outcome:** Accept the criticism and thank your teacher for her help.

Check your defensiveness. It's difficult to hear criticism on something you put a lot of effort into. You may feel the urge to explain why you wrote something, or to prove that her feedback is wrong. But remember that some notes can be helpful. When you meet with your teacher, the purpose of the meeting is not for you to prove you were right; it's to learn from her feedback, even if you may disagree at first.

First, listen. Sometimes it can be hard to listen to feedback because we are busy feeling so bad about being criticized. Remember that her job is to help you learn so that you can do better on your next paper. Show that you are listening and paying attention; if she is showing you something on your paper, look where she is looking. Occasionally glance up to make eye contact and show that you're engaged. This also shows that you are open to hearing her comments.

Ask questions. This is another way of showing that you're interested and open to her feedback. Asking questions also demonstrates that you're ready to learn more and move forward.

Say thanks. As difficult as it might be to hear the criticism, keep in mind that your teacher took the time and energy to read your paper, give you thoughtful feedback, and meet with you to review it. Make sure to thank her by telling her, "Thanks for taking the time to go over this with me," or, "I really appreciate your feedback on this."

Choosing What Works for You

You and your friend are in a rush to get to fourth period. Your friend criticizes you for wanting to take the long way to class. You know there are shorter routes, but this is the way you go every day.

▷ **Desired Outcome:** Acknowledge that he may be right, express yourself, and make a choice about which way to go.

Stay open to new ideas. We all have ways of wanting to do things, and you might be really comfortable walking a certain way to class every day. But does your friend have a point? Would it be a lot quicker to go the other way?

Don't take it personally. Sometimes confrontations escalate because we really want to prove we're right about something. It can feel like a personal attack when someone criticizes how you do things. But in this case, is your friend's criticism personal, or is it a matter of saving time?

Identify what's bothering you. In chapter 7, we discussed how some autistic people like routines. When something interferes with how we expected things to go, it can be really distressing. Does your friend's criticism—his suggestion to go another way—interfere with your expectations and plans for your daily routine? This can feel uncomfortable, as if you are being called out for wanting to do things your way. If your friend doesn't know that you prefer predictability and routines, he may simply be pointing out that there is a quicker way to go. It may be worth explaining to your friend why your routine is important to you.

Express your needs. Explain that doing things the same way each day helps you feel more relaxed, if that's the case. If you don't know this friend well, you can also stick with something vague, like, "Thanks for letting me know the other way is quicker. I guess I'm just used to walking this way."

Make a choice. If you're ready to push out of your comfort zone, try the new route with your friend.

Responding Online

You posted a picture of yourself attending your favorite musical with your cousin. A friend of a friend commented on your picture, "Musicals are boring!"

▷ **Desired Outcome:** Disregard the comment, review online privacy, and move on.

Manage privacy settings. In this case, you might want to double-check who has access to your posts. If people are commenting who you don't really know, make sure to change your privacy settings so that friends of friends can't see posts.

Don't respond. It's never a good idea to get into a debate on social media. You like musicals, and that's all that matters. You are probably not going to convince the commenter that musicals are great by going back and forth online, nor do you need them to be convinced. If you don't know the person who made the comment, you could even delete the comment.

Respond to positive comments. Focus on the positive comments on your post. While everyone can have different tastes, and it's okay if someone doesn't like musicals, it's not okay for someone to criticize you on social media.

It's Okay to Say No

When your peers ask you to do something that you don't want to do, are you comfortable telling them no? If you have a hard time with this, you're not alone. Most people prefer to avoid a confrontation with friends. Maybe we don't want to stand out by not going along with what everyone else is doing. Sometimes we fear that we won't appear cool, or that our peers will reject us. This is especially hard when you are trying to make friends and you want your peers to like you.

But saying no is okay. In fact, it's really important! You don't have to do something just because your friends are doing it. It's important to make your own choices about what's right for you. You need a way of opting out when your peers are asking you to do something you don't want to do, or something that may get you in trouble or even hurt you. Saying no is part of knowing your limits and making independent decisions. It's also a way to assert yourself and your values.

When to Say No

Knowing *when* to say no can be tricky, especially if everyone around you is urging you to do something. So how exactly do you say no when you feel pressured to say yes?

Here are specific times to say no:

You feel unsafe. Anytime you don't feel safe or you think your safety is at risk, say no. For example, a bunch of your friends are piling into a car, and you know there won't be enough seat belts for everyone. If you think an activity or situation is unsafe, it's okay to opt out.

You feel like someone is crossing a boundary. Whether someone is crossing a physical boundary (getting into your space, touching you) or asking you to do something that you're not comfortable with, it's okay to say no.

You're just not comfortable. You don't necessarily need a reason to justify saying no. If something doesn't feel right, don't do it. Trust your gut!

Unreasonable Demands

Let's say your friend is asking you to ditch class with her. You really like her as a friend, so you don't want to disappoint her, but you don't feel comfortable skipping class.

▶ **Desired Outcome:** Clearly say no and suggest an alternative.

Check your emotions. You might be flattered and even excited that your friend asked you to ditch class with her. But the idea of ditching class makes you feel nervous. Experiencing two or more conflicting feelings at the same time can be confusing and maybe even anxiety-provoking. Take a moment to recognize what you are feeling and identify what you are comfortable with.

Say no. When your friend tells you that you both should ditch class together, tell her no, or, "I don't want to miss class." By focusing on not wanting to miss class, you're making your "no" about your values and not about whether you want to hang out with your friend.

Use nonverbal cues. Make sure that when you say no, you aren't smiling and sending a mixed message. Make eye contact and have a neutral or more serious facial expression. This leaves no room for your friend to doubt how you feel.

Suggest something else. You might worry that because you are saying no, your friend won't want to hang out with you, or you might be concerned that you're sending her a message that you don't want to hang out with her. To clear the air, offer an alternative plan. Suggest that you meet up at lunch or after school. For example, "I'm not going to ditch class, but I'd love to hang out later. Meet you at lunch?"

Peer Pressure

Imagine that you're at a friend's house hanging out and your friend offers you his parents' beer or another substance. You've never had it before, and you're curious about it, but you know you shouldn't be having any.

▷ **Desired Outcome:** Say no and continue hanging out.

Say no clearly. Calmly say, "No, thanks." You can also say, "No, it's not my thing." Make sure that you are serious when you say no. Make eye contact, use a neutral expression, and state your response like a fact rather than a question. The more certain you sound, the less likely your friend will continue to ask you.

Give a reason. A close friend may be okay with you simply saying no, and the interaction will end there. If it doesn't, giving a reason or excuse for not drinking can help strengthen your "no" so that your friend stops asking you. It's okay to make up a reason, and it can be helpful to brainstorm ahead of time if you know you're going to be in a situation, like a party, where you might be offered alcohol or another substance. Here are some examples of excuses you can give (Hint: It's okay to blame your parents!): "My parents would ground me for life if they smelled it on my breath!"; "The smell gives me a headache, so I stay away from it"; "I have tryouts in the morning, so I'm taking it easy tonight."

Suggest another activity. Ask your friend to shoot hoops, grab a snack, or play a video game instead.

Go home. If your friend continues to pressure you, even after you've firmly said no, given a reason, and suggested another activity, then you can make an excuse for needing to leave. Again, it's okay to use your parents as an excuse by telling your friend that you have a family dinner or that your parents are texting you to come help out at home. You can also say, "I've gotta run so I can get my homework done. See you at school tomorrow!"

Staying Safe Online

It can feel like you're safe when you're on your computer at home, but being online can make you vulnerable, too. Imagine one of your peers is following you on Instagram. You've seen him around school, but you've never hung out with him. He messages you back and forth a couple of times, and then asks you to send him a revealing picture of yourself. You don't feel comfortable with this.

▷ **Desired Outcome:** Say no and cut off the connection.

Say no clearly. It's important to say no clearly, since nonverbal cues like tone cannot be conveyed online. Do not include any friendly emojis because they could confuse your message. He might not think you're being serious if you're sending a smiley face with your no.

Give a brief explanation, if you want. In this case, it's perfectly fine to say no and stop the chat with no explanation. If you want to say more, you can add, "I'm not comfortable with that."

Be okay with your answer. We sometimes worry about being rude or that someone won't be our friend if we say no. But your safety is more important than other people's feelings. If the other person starts treating you differently, that's unfortunate. But it's not a reason to do something that could be unsafe or make you vulnerable in another way, like having your picture distributed online.

Making Amends

Most of us don't like the thought of someone being upset with us. But it's inevitable that we'll upset someone at some point, whether we mean to or not. If someone confronts you because you upset them, how can you handle it?

Apologizing

An apology is warranted if you did something to hurt or offend someone else. Even if you didn't *mean* to hurt them, it's still important to acknowledge the other person's feelings. When apologizing, don't try to justify what you said or did. You're not trying to win an argument. You are showing that the relationship is important to you by admitting how you contributed to a conflict or misunderstanding.

When you apologize, use nonverbal communication that shows that you mean it. Making eye contact, using a concerned facial expression, and speaking in a slow, calm tone can help. If you apologize too quickly while looking away, you might not come across as sincere.

Let's imagine that you said something offensive to a friend without realizing it. You told your friend that he's obviously not very good at math. He recently failed his last exam, so he's sensitive about the subject and got upset.

▶ **Desired Outcome:** Acknowledge that what you said was hurtful and apologize.

> **Listen to your friend.** Try to understand how he feels about what you said. By listening, you are showing that you care. Listening also helps you understand why someone is upset so you can empathize with them.

> **Use open body language.** Your body language can convey a lot about your feelings. Even if you feel hesitant to apologize at first, avoid crossing your arms, rolling your eyes, or turning away from your friend. These behaviors can come across as defensive.

Acknowledge their perspective. You can show that you understand your friend's perspective by saying, "I can see why you were offended when I said that," or, "I understand why you're hurt."

Don't try to prove your point. You might be thinking to yourself, "Well, he failed his exam, so I was just telling the truth when I said he wasn't good at math." But sometimes pointing things out, even if they are truthful, can be unnecessarily hurtful. It's best to admit that you shouldn't have said what you did, rather than trying to convince your friend that your comment was okay to make.

Say sorry. It doesn't matter if you think your comment was okay or right. Either way, you hurt your friend's feelings, so make sure to apologize.

An apology is more meaningful when you specify what you are sorry for: "I'm sorry for making a hurtful comment," or, "I'm sorry for hurting you."

If You Let Someone Down

You forgot to meet your friend at lunch. The two of you had texted earlier that day about meeting, but something distracted you, and you didn't show up.

▷ **Desired Outcome:** Acknowledge your mistake and make a new plan for the next day.

Agree with your friend. If your friend tells you that it was uncool of you to leave her hanging at lunch, acknowledge the mistake. Tell her she's right. If she asks what happened, briefly explain ("I ran into a teacher"). You don't need to go into detail.

Empathize. Imagine how it would feel if you were waiting for a friend who never showed up. You'd probably feel hurt, irritated, or embarrassed. Tell your friend that you understand how she must have felt by expressing one of these feelings ("You must have felt confused when I didn't show.").

Say sorry. Apologize for leaving her hanging.

Make new plans. Ask your friend if she would be willing to reschedule for the next day—and tomorrow, make sure to follow through!

Depending on how upset she is, she may not be open to another meetup. But it's important to ask, because doing so shows that you're motivated to hang out and make up for the mistake.

When Not to Apologize

Since apologizing can defuse tension, sometimes we use it too often to make sure we aren't causing any misunderstandings. You might say sorry a lot to avoid conflict.

But apologizing too often might make you seem less sincere when you do apologize. If you apologize all the time, others find it harder to know when you really mean it. Constantly apologizing can also make you appear less confident in your opinions and actions.

Accepting an Apology

When you accept a friend's apology, you accept that they feel regret, care about your feelings, and will be thoughtful about how to handle a similar situation in the future. Accepting an apology can strengthen a relationship.

Take the apology seriously if you think the other person really means it. Saying something like, "It's fine," without making eye contact might show that it's really *not* fine, or that you are too annoyed or hurt to really accept the apology.

If a friend apologizes but continues doing hurtful things, you don't have to keep accepting their apologies. You might decide that you can't trust your friend to change their behavior. In that case, it might be time to find different people to hang out with. Here are some specific examples of accepting an apology.

Setting Expectations

Let's say your sister borrowed your shirt without asking.

▶ **Desired Outcome:** You want to listen to your sister and accept her apology. Then you want to express what was upsetting and how you would like things to go differently next time.

"Thank you for apologizing. I appreciate that. I was just annoyed that you didn't ask me first. Next time, please ask."

"I appreciate it. You know you can borrow my clothes. Just check with me next time."

"No worries—can you ask me next time you want to borrow something?"

Showing Appreciation

Your friend said something that hurt your feelings.

▶ **Desired Outcome:** You want to first listen to your friend. Then you want to accept their apology and let them know that you appreciate them trying to understand what was hurtful.

"Thank you. I appreciate you trying to understand why it hurt."

"It's okay. Sounds like it was a misunderstanding."

"I appreciate the apology."

After apologizing or accepting an apology, it's time to move forward. It's natural to still feel a little hurt, even after the apology. In fact, it's okay to tell your friend that you accept their apology but need a little time to process everything, especially if you were really hurt. Don't take too long, though, and don't ignore them, or they might think that you are too upset to continue being friends.

Making Up

Once apologies have been given and accepted, try to let things go. Don't keep bringing up the situation or reminding your friend what they did wrong. Letting go helps you move forward with the friendship by staying in touch or making plans.

If you aren't sure if your friend has let something go and is ready to move on, ask them directly. For example, ask, "Are you good?" or, "Are we okay?" Here are some specific ways to move forward after an apology.

Expressing How You Feel

Let's say your friend apologized to you for not showing up to your birthday party. You are still hurt, but you can see that her apology is sincere.

▷ **Desired Outcome:** You want to express how her actions made you feel. Then you want to accept her apology and find a way to move on.

Friend: "I'm sorry I wasn't there. I should have at least texted. My mom asked me to watch my brother at the last minute."

You: "Thanks for explaining. I was just super bummed you weren't there, and I felt like you flaked."

Friend: "I can see why you were hurt. I am so sorry. I didn't want to miss it. Can I make it up to you by taking you to lunch tomorrow?"

You: "I appreciate the apology. Yes, let's try for tomorrow."

Showing You're Listening

Imagine that you apologized to your friend for yelling during a heated discussion. He was offended and didn't want to talk to you after being yelled at.

▷ **Desired Outcome:** You want to give a sincere apology and show your friend that you can chat in a calm and respectful way.

Friend: "I can't even talk to you when you're like this."

You: (still speaking loudly) "I'm sorry. I shouldn't have yelled. I just got so worked up talking about this!"

Friend: "I don't want to be yelled at."

You: (using a calmer, quieter voice) "You're right. That wasn't fair to you. Let's take a breather and try again. I promise not to yell this time."

Friend: "Sounds good. I'm up for that. Thanks."

▶ **REFLECTION QUESTIONS**

- Has your own defensiveness made confrontations escalate in the past?
- Can you think of something you've done that has upset someone else? Knowing what you know now, how would you handle that situation differently?
- What are some of your core values, and how can they help you say no in the future?

CHAPTER NINE

RESPONDING TO BULLYING

Unfortunately, bullying is a reality for many kids and teens today. Autistic people can be targets of bullying, especially if they spend more time on their own without a group of peers to provide a social buffer against bullying. Other people who are perceived as being different can also become targets. If you have been bullied before, it's not your fault, and it doesn't mean you've done anything wrong. *No one* deserves to be bullied. In this chapter, you'll get strategies to help you handle different kinds of bullying if they ever happen to you.

- Have you ever been bullied before? How did it make you feel?
- If you have been bullied before, what strategies have helped?
- What strategies haven't helped?

What Is Bullying?

Bullying is when someone uses words or actions to purposefully hurt another person. How do you know the difference between bullying and other types of conflict, or even between bullying and when teens are just giving each other a hard time? Here are some ways we know that someone's behavior is bullying:

Deliberate. If someone accidentally bumps into you in the hallway, that's not bullying, but if someone pushes you on purpose, that might be.

Ongoing. When a person repeatedly targets you by acting aggressively, it's bullying. Making fun of your last name once might be a one-time incident, but intimidating, taunting, or insulting you over and over again is bullying.

Imbalance of power. The person doing the bullying has more physical power or social influence and uses that power imbalance to victimize you. In other words, they are bigger or stronger, or have a group of friends backing them up.

Are You Being Bullied?

So how can you tell if you're being bullied? Here are some signs you can look for:

Physical harm. If someone is hurting you by repeatedly hitting, kicking, pushing, or otherwise being physical with you (like hair pulling or grabbing your clothing or backpack), you are likely being bullied.

Verbal taunts. Even if you are never physically harmed, repeated teasing causes long-lasting emotional pain. If someone repeatedly yells at, mocks, or draws attention to you in negative ways, these words can hurt. Criticisms based on gender, sexuality, race, beliefs, appearance, and size are forms of aggression and may make you feel unsafe or alone.

Nonverbal taunts. If someone mimics you, uses offensive gestures toward you, or threatens you by showing you what they would do to you (like clenching a fist when you look at them), this might also be bullying if it happens consistently and makes you feel unsafe.

Fear. Do you feel scared around certain people? Are you afraid to go places where certain people might be? Pay attention to your fear and what it might be trying to tell you.

If you feel threatened physically or emotionally on a regular basis, ask yourself if someone might be making you feel this way.

Cyberbullying

Bullying doesn't have to happen in person. One type of bullying, where someone sends hurtful messages or posts harmful content, is cyberbullying. It can happen through texts, email, or on social media. The messages, photos, or posts share negative, harmful, or mean information about someone else. The information is not necessarily true, but it usually makes the person feel embarrassed or humiliated.

People sending or posting these messages may feel bolder than they would when interacting with someone in person because they don't have to experience the immediate consequences of someone else's reaction. Posting a mean comment feels easier than saying it to someone's face. People who post hurtful messages anonymously may think they don't have to take any personal responsibility for their actions.

RUMORS AND GOSSIP

A **rumor** is any information spread about a person that may or may not be true. When someone spreads rumors, they can turn into **gossip**, or details about a person that might be surprising or personal.

Sometimes we feel like we are bonding with a friend over gossip. It's like trading secrets, and can bring people closer together when they share an opinion about another person. But ultimately, a friendship cannot be based on gossiping about others. If your friend often reveals private or provocative information about someone else, can you trust that they would keep your information private if you confide in them?

People who create rumors or spread gossip may do it to get attention, feel like they belong, or feel more powerful than someone else.

When someone spreads gossip about you, you might have the urge to respond right away by setting the record straight or spreading an equally bad rumor about them. But it's best to distance yourself and stay neutral. Confronting the gossiper can lead to more conflict.

Instead, try the following tips from Dr. Elizabeth Laugeson's *The Science of Making Friends*:

- Acknowledge the rumor: "Did you hear that Jim thinks I got an A because I *cheated*?"
- Comment about how ridiculous or even humorous the situation is: "*Right,* so apparently I have cheated on every exam in high school to get straight As?"
- Act surprised that anyone would even believe it: "I'm amazed that people believe it!"

This shows that you are not bothered by the gossip, and that you think it absurd that anyone would think the information is true.

Dealing with a Bully

Depending on the situation, it's important to respond to a bully directly, or get help in order to protect yourself. If you don't address the bullying in some way, the bully may think it's okay to continue. If you are being physically hurt, seek support from an adult rather than trying to fight the bully. Let's explore how best to respond based on the type of bullying you're experiencing.

Verbal Bullying

Verbal bullying refers to repeated name-calling, taunting, and teasing. Though verbal bullying doesn't cause physical harm, it can cause feelings of sadness, loneliness, and damage to your self-esteem. Verbal bullying is usually less obvious than physical bullying. It can be harder for others to notice it, making it hard to get help. Here are some tips for handling verbal bullying:

Don't ignore it. You may have heard that you should ignore someone who is teasing or insulting you. Unfortunately, research has shown that this doesn't work. Walking away or ignoring the verbal bullying before you give a response usually leads to continued teasing. (The bully is looking for a reaction, so they may keep trying until they get one from you.)

Don't tattle (but do get advice). Getting advice from a trusted adult is important. You don't have to keep the verbal bullying a secret. Getting bullied is not your fault, and it is not anything to be ashamed of. However, telling on the bully could lead to more teasing.

Check your emotions. When someone verbally bullies you, it hurts. But since bullies tease in order to get you to react, try not to show too much emotion by looking hurt or upset. Show them that it doesn't bother you by using a neutral facial expression or even a subtle smile.

Use a short phrase as a comeback. In *The Science of Making Friends*, Dr. Laugeson suggests thinking of some brief comebacks ahead of time, like, "Whatever," or, "Oh, okay," to show that you aren't bothered. Your tone should be casual without a lot of emotion. In addition to using a neutral facial expression, try shrugging and looking away to show that it isn't a big deal.

Walk away. At this point, now that you have responded, you can walk away.

Resist the urge to engage in any more conversation or verbal exchange. Doing so just gives the bully more opportunities to get a rise out of you.

Social Bullying

Social bullying happens when you have been repeatedly and purposefully excluded from a group, or when a friend tries to turn other friends against you—such as by encouraging others not to include you in plans, or starting a rumor to prevent others from hanging out with you. This might happen behind your back, making it harder to know when it's happening. It can also happen in front of you if someone tries to embarrass you or make you look bad in front of your peers. Either way, you end up feeling isolated, sad, and less socially accepted. Here's what you can do to deal with a social bully:

Evaluate your friends. Acknowledging that your friend isn't really a friend can be painful. But if someone is purposefully leaving you out or trying to get others to turn against you, they aren't a friend you can trust.

Face the truth. Being socially bullied is not your fault. But consider whether you did anything to upset your friend. If you did, own up to it and apologize. You might not want to stay friends, but clearing the air can help stop the bullying.

It may not be about you. Often, social bullying is more about the bully than it is about you. Your friend might be a social bully even if you are the greatest friend ever. Social bullies tend to create toxic environments, probably because they feel threatened or need to find a way to control the situation and the friend group. They lash out to try to make themselves look or feel better, without caring about how they're hurting other people.

Distance yourself. When friends turn into bullies, you may not want to invest in the friendship anymore. This can be really difficult, especially if the social bullying has caused your peer group to leave you out. Don't engage in text messaging or conversations with them. One of your other friends from the group may reach out to you at some point, but distancing yourself is important so that you don't contribute to the social drama and add more fuel to the fire.

Seek healthy friendships. Being a target of social bullying sometimes forces us to seek new, trustworthy friends. This can take time, but having friends who will support you rather than try to tear you down is worth the effort.

Physical Bullying

Physical bullying is when someone is trying to harm your body or invade your personal space. This ranges from subtler behaviors like tripping you or flinging trash at you to more serious actions like pushing, hitting, kicking, and punching.

Physical bullying can also include destroying your things, like ripping your clothing or damaging your phone. If you have ever experienced any of these actions, you know that they can be terrifying and humiliating. Here are some tips you can use to handle physical bullying:

Ask for help. If you are being threatened or physically harmed, always tell a trusted teacher, coach, school staff member like a counselor, or parent. But do it discreetly (not in front of the bully or other peers). This is not a time to tattle on the bully's other misbehaviors you may have witnessed (like if they ditched class). The focus is on your safety and letting an adult know if you are in danger.

Avoid. You don't need to rearrange your entire life around avoiding the bully, but also remember that if they're not near you, they cannot attack you. If you can just as easily choose to walk a route that doesn't take you past the bully, wait in line a few people away from them, or go to the bathroom when they're not already in there, do so.

Create a buddy system. If you *do* need to be physically close to your bully, you are less of a target when you are with someone else or with a group of people. You're also likely to feel more confident. Whenever possible, surround yourself with others, especially if you know you may run into a bully.

Walk away. If you still end up seeing or running into your bully, calmly walk away.

Use your body language. A bully tries to have power over the person they're bullying. When you move away from a bully, walk with your head up and shoulders back, showing confidence. Show that the bully doesn't really bother you (even if they do!).

Don't provoke. In the section on verbal bullying (page 133), using comebacks was discussed. But when it comes to physical aggression, it's best not to provoke a bully. Don't give bullies any excuse to hurt you.

Don't fight back. Unless you have no choice but to defend yourself physically, make a point of removing yourself from a situation rather than adding to it by fighting back. Fighting back can get dangerous, and it puts you in the position of being partly responsible for the violence. It may encourage the bully to come after you again.

Handling a Cyberbully

Cyberbullying can happen 24 hours a day, since it happens electronically. The fact that it can happen anytime makes avoiding a cyberbully a challenge. Here are some ways to deal with online bullying behaviors.

Before you engage with a cyberbully, check your **privacy settings**. Keeping your social media and other accounts private is the first step in preventing cyberbullying from ever starting. Privacy settings limit the number of people who have access to your profiles. Make sure that you have to give permission for people to follow you or add you as a friend.

Block and delete. If someone targets you online, block or delete them from your accounts so that they no longer have access to your posts. Some social media platforms allow you to report inappropriate comments.

Don't respond. Since bullies want attention and want a reaction from you, don't engage. Ignore or delete their comments and resist the urge to get into debates or arguments online. Going back and forth online just escalates the situation. Remember that everything online is permanent, including your responses.

Save evidence. If you're being bullied online, print out the exchanges or take screenshots. By keeping copies of everything, you have proof of what happened that you can show to adults who can help.

Ask for help. Cyberbullying is serious. If you are being targeted repeatedly, make sure to tell an adult like your parent or a teacher. They can help you figure out if the cyberbullying needs to be reported to a principal, or even the police, if there are threats to your or someone else's safety.

Keep private information private. Never share personal information like your address online. (See chapter 3 to review what's private and public information.) A cyberbully can use that information to hurt you.

Asking for Help

It's always okay to let your parents or another trusted adult know what's going on. This is especially important if you are being physically hurt or if your safety is threatened in some way. **When you're feeling unsafe, *always* let a trusted adult know.** Your safety comes first.

Even if the bullying is not physical, you need support. Make sure to talk to a trusted teacher, counselor, or parent—they might have gone through something similar and might be able to help you with great advice. Asking for support is different from telling on your peers. You can always ask for advice without telling them who the bully is.

But if your strategies or the adults' advice is not stopping the bully, then let the staff at school (or camp, work, or wherever the bullying is happening) know who the bully is so that they can help keep you safe. Talking to someone about bullying is a sign of strength. It's a way to take control and protect yourself.

▶ **REFLECTION QUESTIONS**

- What would you do if you saw someone else being physically bullied?
- What would you do if someone repeatedly made rude comments on your social media posts?
- How would you decide when it's time to tell a teacher or counselor about a bully at school?

CONCLUSION

Congratulations on finishing the book! The strategies you learned here will make up some of the tools in your social survival tool kit. You can use whichever tools you want, whenever they might be helpful. With these tools, you can face new social situations with more confidence.

Building social skills and friendships takes practice. This can be intimidating or discouraging at first, but the more you do it, the more comfortable you will feel. Don't forget to check in on your own emotions, take breaks, and recharge on your own using the tools you learned.

Healthy friendships give you a sense of connectedness and community. Friends can be some of your biggest cheerleaders. But you have a lot to offer your friends, too, and other people are eager to get to know you. Your differences are what make you unique and interesting. Let other people see and celebrate who you are.

Remember that you can connect with people when *you* feel ready. No one can tell you how much you should socialize, with whom you should become friends, or how many relationships you should have. You have the power to build and enjoy friendships on your own terms.

RESOURCES

The ASD Independence Workbook: Transition Skills for Teens and Young Adults with Autism by Francis Tabone

The Awesome Autistic Go-To Guide: A Practical Handbook for Autistic Teens and Tweens by Yenn Purkis and Tanya Masterman

AWKWARD: The Social Dos and Don'ts of Being a Young Adult by Katie Saint and Carlos Torres

The Guide to Good Mental Health on the Autism Spectrum by Jeanette Purkis, Emma Goodall, and Jane Nugent

It's Raining Cats and Dogs: An Autism Spectrum Guide to the Confusing World of Idioms, Metaphors, and Everyday Expressions by Michael Barton

Living Well on the Spectrum: How to Use Your Strengths to Meet the Challenges of Asperger Syndrome/High-Functioning Autism by Valerie Gaus

The Mindfulness Journal for Teens: Prompts and Practices to Help You Stay Cool, Calm, and Present by Jennie Marie Battistin

Overcoming Anxiety and Depression on the Autism Spectrum: A Self-Help Guide Using CBT by Lee A. Wilkinson

Parties, Dorms, and Social Norms: A Crash Course in Safe Living for Young Adults on the Autism Spectrum by Lisa Meeks and Tracy Loye Masterson

The Science of Making Friends: Helping Socially Challenged Teens and Young Adults by Elizabeth Laugeson

Smile & Succeed for Teens: A Crash Course in Face-to-Face Communication by Kirt Manecke

Uniquely Human: A Different Way of Seeing Autism by Barry Prizant

INDEX

Fight or flight response, 54–55
Figurative language, 38–41
Flexibility, 100–101
Friends
  being left out by, 109
  disagreements with, 102–103, 104
  vs. followers, 6
  importance of, 4
  making plans with, 92–94, 103–104
  mistakes made by, 8
  qualities of, 4–5, 6–7
  roles of, 7–8

G

Gossip, 132
Grandin, Temple, 12
Greetings, 22–23, 84

H

Hand gestures, 18
Hanging out, 92–94
Happiness, 56
Honesty, 36–37
Humor, 20. *See also* Sarcasm
Hyperbole, 40

I

Inside jokes, 20
Interest, expressing, 82–83
Irony, 38–39

J

Joining in
  activities, 88–90
  approaching others, 83–86
  entering conversations, 87–88
  expressing interest, 82–83
  knowing when to, 78–81
  parties, 90–91
Jokes, 20

L

Laugeson, Elizabeth, 132, 134
Listening, 27–28, 61, 126–127
Littering, 105–106

M

Mirroring
  body language, 17–18
  greetings, 22
  personal space, 21–22
Mistakes
  letting someone down, 123–124
  made by friends, 8

N

Names, learning, 82–83
Negative thoughts, 68–71
"No," saying, 118–121

O

Online etiquette
  critical comments, 117–118
  cyberbullying, 131, 137–138
  email, 44–45
  importance of, 41–42
  privacy, 46, 48, 137–138
  safety, 121
  social media, 45–47
  texting, 42–44
Opinions, 114–115

P

Parties, 90–91
Peer pressure, 120–121
Peers. *See also* Friends
  approaching others, 83–86
  expressing interest, 82–83
  joining in with, 78–81
Personal information, 48
Personal space, 20–22

Plans
  changes to, 103–104
  making, 91–94
Posture, 16, 17–18
Privacy, 46, 48, 137–138

R

Rhetorical questions/comments, 35–36
Routines, changes to, 98–102
Rule breakers, 105–108
Rumors, 132

S

Sadness, 56
Safe spaces, 72
Safety. *See also* Bullying
  online, 121
  saying "no," 118–119
  stimming, 72–73
Sarcasm, 38–40, 41
Saying what you mean, not, 34–37
Science of Making Friends, The
  (Laugeson), 132, 134
Self-stimulatory behavior, 71–73
Self-talk, 68–71
Sensitive topics, 30

Slang, 40
Social media
  critical comments, 117–118
  cyberbullying, 131, 137–138
  etiquette, 45–47
  friends vs. followers, 6
  safety, 121
Spamming, 43–44
Stimming, 71–73
Stimuli, 56–57
Stressors, 55

T

Tattling, 108
Texting, 42–44
Thoughts, negative, 68–71, 87–88, 89
Tone of voice, 19
Touch, 18–19
Triggers, 56–57

V

Volume, of voice, 19

W

White lies, 36–37

ACKNOWLEDGMENTS

First, thank you to my editor, Annie Choi, for her insight, direction, thoughtful feedback, and patience throughout the writing of this book.

Siblings are often our first introduction to negotiating our social world with peers. Thank you to my brother, Adam Sterling, for deepening my understanding; you inspired me to be a more compassionate and effective clinician.

My clients and their families fed my brain with ideas and inspiration prior to and during the writing of this book. We worked through various social dilemmas together, and I was able to draw on these discussions to inform my writing. Thank you for trusting me with this delicate role in walking through these situations, which has allowed me to fully understand and appreciate your unique strengths as we problem-solve. I have learned from you as I hope you have from me.

This book was written during the COVID-19 shutdown. Writing a book about social interaction while social distancing was a challenging and ironic undertaking, but also forced me to consider the elements of socialization that really are essential for relationships. Add to that the dynamic of being home with my family throughout the writing of this book; my husband and our two boys were subject to my writing schedule and brainstorming ideas for social scenarios. Thank you to my husband for your support and encouragement, and for entertaining two rambunctious boys while I wrote. Thanks to our kids for understanding when Mommy had to work, and for your curiosity and excitement about the final product, which you eagerly hoped to see.

ABOUT THE AUTHOR

Lindsey Sterling, PhD, is a clinical psychologist specializing in ASD and coexisting conditions, including anxiety and depression. She earned her BS in psychobiology from UCLA and her MS/PhD in child clinical psychology from the University of Washington. She completed her clinical internship in developmental disabilities at the UCLA Semel Institute for Neuroscience and Human Behavior.

During her postdoctoral fellowship at UCLA, Dr. Sterling was awarded funding from the National Institutes of Health to conduct research on the physiology of anxiety among autistic youth. Her academic positions have included clinical faculty in the UCLA Department of Psychiatry, staff psychologist at the UCLA Child and Adult Neurodevelopmental Clinic, interim professor and director of the Autism Center at Claremont McKenna College, and tenure-track professor in the Department of Psychology, California State University Long Beach.

Dr. Sterling continues to work with autistic individuals and their families through her private practices in Long Beach and Newport Beach, California.

Printed in the USA
CPSIA information can be obtained
at www.ICGtesting.com
LVHW050745171223
766457LV00005B/43